Divorce Mediation Manual

Stanley L. Bartelmie

Order this book online at www.trafford.com
or email orders@trafford.com

Most Trafford titles are also available at major online book retailers.

Printed in the United States of America.

ISBN: 978-1-4269-6176-2 (sc)
ISBN: 978-1-4269-6177-9 (e)

Library of Congress Control Number: 2011904423

Trafford rev. 03/29/2011

 www.trafford.com

North America & international
toll-free: 1 888 232 4444 (USA & Canada)
phone: 250 383 6864 ♦ fax: 812 355 4082

Authors Page

Stanley L. Bartelmie, JD, CFLS, ACFLS, has been practicing in Santa Clara County, California for more than 30 years in the areas of family law, trusts, trust administration and probate. Stan is a member of the Mediation and Arbitration panels with the Santa Clara County Superior Court. Stan received formal mediation training from Nancy Foster, JD and Jessica Notini, JD at the Northern California Mediation Center. For more than 15 years, Stan's practice has been focused on mediation.

I wish to acknowledge and thank C. Nancy Sallan, mediator. For several years, Nancy and I developed a co-mediation process for divorcing couples, providing a unique gender-neutral mediation platform.

Finally, my wife, Toni Lama-Raad, has provided strong support and direction for the development of this manual. She has devoted hours to reviewing, correcting, and providing suggestions. All of these acts were instrumental for the completion of this self-help guide. I love you.

THE DIVORCE MEDIATION MANUAL

TABLE OF CONTENTS

Page

Chapter 1	What is Mediation?	1
	Styles of Mediation	6
	A. Facilitative Method	6
	B. Evaluative Method	6
	C. Transformative	7
	D. Caucus	7
Chapter 2	Comparing the Different Approaches when Terminating the Marriage	9
	A. Take It To Court . . . The Litigation Approach	10
	B. The Collaboration Approach	14
	C. The Mediation Approach	17
Chapter 3	Why Choose Mediation?	19
	A. The Impact of Divorce Upon Children	23
Chapter 4	When is Mediation likely to Succeed?	25
	A. Suggestions For Better Communication	28
	B. Tips For Productive Dialog	31
Chapter 5	When is Mediation likely to fail?	35
Chapter 6	Choosing a mediator	39
	A. Some Questions for the Mediator	41
Chapter 7	What Obligations does the Mediator owe to the Parties?	45
	A. Explanation of the Mediation Process	47
	B. Procedural Fairness	47
	C. Confidentiality	48
	D. Diligence	48
	E. Impartiality	49

F.   Representation and other Professional Services 49

G. Recommending Other Services 50

H. The Interests of Non-participants 50

I.   Settlement Agreements..50

J.   Discretionary Termination and Withdrawal 51

K. Manner of Withdrawal..51

L.   Truthfulness 51

M. Solicitation of Business..52

N. Compensation and Gift..52

O. Complaint Procedure 53

Chapter 8   The Importance of determining The Date of Separation 55

Chapter 9   General Legal Concepts for Property Division.........................59

A. Separate or Community Property?................................60

B. Three Concepts for Dividing Property..........................62

C. How will the parties determine the Character of their property?......62

D. How will the parties Value their property? 63

E. How will the parties divide their property?..................64

Chapter 10 Real Estate...69

A. Real Estate and Different Ways to Divide the Family Residence 70

B. Deferring the Sale of the Family Residence...................70

Chapter 11 Employee Benefits 83

A. What are Employee Benefits? 84

B. Dividing Stock Options 87

Chapter 12 Personal Property 91

A. Dividing Personal Property..92

B. Tips For Dividing Personal Property............................93

Chapter 13 Child Custody and Parenting 95

A. How Do We Tell the Children about the Divorce? 96

B. Determining Child Custody...98

  C. Parenting and Time Share Agreements 101

  D. Parenting After the Divorce..105

  E. Creating a Closer Relationship with Your Child 106

  F. Guidelines For Parents To Help Diminish Conflict 107

  G. Co-Parenting Tips 108

  H. Ten Tips for Co-Parenting..109

  I. More Considerations for Co-Parenting...110

Chapter 14 Support 113

  A. Calculating a Child Support Amount...114

  B. Calculating a Spousal Support Amount...117

  C. Calculating a Family Support Amount 120

  D. Registered Domestic Partners 121

Chapter 15 A Divorce Mediation Model..123

  A. First Mediation Session (1 to 2 hours) 124

  B. Second Mediation Session (1 to 2 hours).......................................127

  C. Third Mediation Session (1 to 2 hours) 130

  D. Fourth Mediation Session (1 to 2 hours) 132

  E. Fifth Mediation Session (1 to 2 hours) 134

  F. Sixth Mediation Session (1 to 2 hours)..136

APPENDIX

Books for Parents...139

Books for 3 to 5 Year Olds 142

Books for 6 to 9 Year Olds 142

Books for 10 to 12 Year Olds..142

Books for 13 to 17 Year Olds 143

Web Sites...143

Audio Programs 144

RESOURCES

Page

Chapter 1-3..145

Chapter 4-9..146

Chapter 10-13..147

Chapter 14-15..148

CHAPTER 1

WHAT IS MEDIATION?

"I can win an argument on any topic, against any opponent.
People know this, and steer clear of me at parties. Often, as
a sign of their great respect, they don't even invite me."

Dave Barry

This manual is meant to positively assist, inform, and navigate couples engaged in the process of divorce mediation.

Divorce mediation is about you, and your soon to be ex-spouse, choosing what to do when you are coming apart, and deciding what is best for both of you.

If there are children, then the mediation process can become an important process to promote a healthy connection between the parents and the children.

In mediation, you and your spouse meet with a neutral third party, the mediator, and with his or her help, you work through the issues you need to resolve, so the two of you can end your marriage together peacefully, respectfully, and inexpensively.

The basic topics to resolve in mediation include the following:

(1) Division of Assets and Debts

(2) Child Custody and Establishing a Parenting Plan

(3) Child Support, Spousal Support or Family Support

(4) Division of Employee/Retirement Benefits

(5) Resolving Reimbursement Claims

(6) Avoiding Taxes and Defining the Tax Basis of Assets to be divided

The manual provides you with a basic tool for you to review when considering a divorce or engaged in divorce mediation.

You will find a comparison of the <u>Litigated</u> approach, <u>Collaborative</u> approach, and <u>Mediation</u> approach in this manual. Emphasis here is on the Mediation approach.

The information in the Manual can be reviewed when you have questions about property, custody, parenting and support.

You may wish to review the manual to determine if mediation is a process you may wish to choose to end your marriage.

I have been able to find some different definitions of the mediation process, which may prove helpful to the understanding of the term mediation.

"Mediation is the next step beyond direct negotiations and is an alternative to unnecessarily costly, time consuming, and complex court proceedings." California Practice Guide (2010): Alternative Dispute Resolution at 3:5.

"There is a better way to settle differences than a costly courtroom battle. You can control the decisions that affect your family, your finances, your business and your life through mediation, a voluntary settlement process. A mediator is an impartial person who helps people in conflict make practical, informed decisions to resolve the issues before them." Academy of Family Mediators, 1993.

"Mediation is a process in which a neutral third person or persons facilitate communication and negotiations between disputants to assist them in reaching a mutually acceptable agreement, or a better understanding of each participant's interests, needs, values and options." The California Dispute Resolution Council

"A negotiation facilitated by a neutral third party."

David Grappo, a retired Oakland attorney

"A method of non-binding dispute resolution involving a neutral third party who tries to help the disputing parties reach a mutually agreeable solution." Black's Law Dictionary, Second Pocket Edition, Bryan A. Garner, Editor, West Group "Mediation means a process in which a neutral person or persons facilitate communication between disputants to assist them in reaching a mutually acceptable agreement." California Rules of Court, Rule 1580 (c).

"Mediation can be defined as the process by which disputants attempt to reach a consensual settlement of issues in dispute with the assistance and facilitation of a neutral resource person or persons.

At the very least, the process consists of systematically isolating points of agreement and disagreement, developing options, and considering accommodations. The most generic way to look at mediation is to see it as a goal-directed, problem-solving, helping intervention. The goal is to help the parties to resolve their dispute and to reduce the conflict between them. Perhaps a distinction should be made between the ostensible dispute and the underlying conflict. Even if all elements of the dispute cannot be resolved, the conflict can be reduced to a manageable level. However, resolution of the dispute does not always eliminate the conflict. Thus, some refer to mediation as a process not of dispute resolution but of conflict management. Both labels are compatible with the definition proposed here."

Divorce Mediation: Readings, American Bar Association, Leonard L. Riskin, Editor

"Mediation is generally defined as the intervention in a negotiation or a conflict of an acceptable third party who has limited or no authoritative decision-making power but who assists the involved parties in voluntarily reaching a mutually acceptable settlement of issues in dispute. In addition to addressing substantive issues, mediation may also establish or strengthen relationships of trust and respect between the parties or terminate relationships in a manner that minimizes costs and psychological harm."

The Mediation Process, Christopher W. Moore, Jossey-Bass Publishers, San Francisco "Mediation is a forum or meeting in which an impartial person, the mediator, facilitates communication between parties to promote reconciliation, settlement, or understanding among them. A mediator may not impose their own judgment on the issues for that of the parties."

Brian James, "What is Divorce Mediation," © Resourceful Internet Solutions, Inc.

"Mediation is a family-centered conflict resolution process in which an impartial third party assists the participants to negotiate a consensual and informed settlement. In mediation, whether private or public, decision-making authority rests with the parties. The role of the mediator includes reducing the obstacles to communication, maximizing the exploration of alternatives, and addressing the needs of those it is agreed are involved or affected." Academy of Family Mediators, Standards of Practice, 1988 "Me*di*a*tion n 1: private, voluntary process in which an impartial person facilitates communication between parties to promote settlement, 2: does not involve a decision by the mediator."

Southern California Mediation Association.

<u>Styles of Mediation</u>

"Disputes between parties can involve three different kinds of possible outcomes or combinations of outcomes: (1) Distribution of something of value; (2) A mutually acceptable solution to a shared problem; or, (3) Repair of a damaged relationship." James R. Holbrook

A. Facilitative Approach: A facilitative mediator would help promote communication between the parties to help them find an acceptable resolution of their dispute. This style is very effective for custody and creating a parenting plan. The facilitative style of mediation provides enhanced communication and clarification of communication between the parties so that they can solve their own problems.

B. Evaluative Approach: An evaluative mediator would be the person who would express an opinion, suggest different options, and provide some direction for the parties to consider about the different aspects of the dispute to help the parties reach a mutually acceptable agreement. This approach can be effective for the division of assets and debts, as well as, the resolution of reimbursement claims. The evaluative mediator assumes that the parties need some direction based upon the law, and standards in the practice or technology. She or he should be qualified to give such direction based on experience, education, training and objectivity.

C. Transformative Approach: This style has emphasis on preserving or enhancing the relationship between the parties, and the parties are empowered to solve their conflict with an emphasis on mutual respect.

D. Caucus Approach: In the mediation process it may become necessary to meet separately with the parties to help with evaluation and understanding, and to help the parties reach agreement. This may be effective if there is a domestic violence restraining order in place, or a history of domestic violence. The parties agree whether everything that is said in a caucus is Confidential. Or, you agree in advance that everything said in the caucus shall be disclosed, unless you agree you can tell the mediator not to disclose specific information. A good mediator will be able to freely use these styles of mediation to assist and guide the parties to resolution of their disputes.

CHAPTER 2

COMPARING THE DIFFERENT APPROACHES WHEN TERMINATING THE MARRIAGE

"People are always blaming their circumstances for what they are. I don't believe in circumstances. The people who get on in this world are the people who get up and look for the circumstances they want, and, if they can't find them, make them."

George Bernard Shaw

<u>Take It To Court . . . The Litigation Approach</u>

This is the adversarial approach, and it involves an Attorney-Client relationship (Husband vs. Wife and Wife vs. Husband).

In this model, personal confidences and private information often get disclosed to gain an advantage over the other spouse.

This approach depends on information that supports one side and discredits the other side.

It involves public exposure of personal financial information at a court hearing or court trial.

Attorneys will gather personal information by using Interrogatories (a list of written questions to be answered by a party in the divorce proceeding under penalty of perjury); Subpoenas (a notice requiring production of documents from a third-party and/or third-party's oral testimony under penalty of perjury); Depositions (questions propounded to a party or an expert witness, in a divorce proceeding, in the presence of a certified reporter). These are some of the tools used by attorneys to obtain information in a divorce case.

Generally, the issues are framed, defined, and developed, or at least strongly influenced by the attorney. The client, and the client's wishes become the focus for the attorney with very little independent thought for the best interests of the children of the marriage, or the on-going family connection between the parties.

The discovery process and procedures take time to complete and are very expensive. The common progression starts with a court appearance to establish temporary orders for support, custody and visitation. This is followed by the discovery process, which is the gathering of information about assets, debts, income, custody & visitation, and reimbursement claims.

There is often a need to pay for experts to prepare appraisals and reports to help the parties determine the value of assets, vocational opportunities, division of specific assets, custody of the children, and a defined parenting plan.

Court appearances may include Case Management Conferences and Settlement Conferences, and eventually a Trial on unresolved issues. This process will cause a substantial delay in settlement or the resolution of the issues between the parties, and will more likely polarize each party, and inflame emotions between the parties.

The predictable result of this approach is the enormous financial and emotional strain placed on the parties.

The parties are polarized as the result of focusing on the past conduct of each party. Blame, mistrust and revenge often define the focus in the litigation approach.

Communication between the parties tends to be strained, emotional, minimal or non-existent due to this polarity. The relationship of divorcing parents to their children in this model may be defined by "conflict" creating divided loyalties and often results in adjustment problems with the children.

Child custody disputes often require expensive psychological evaluations of parents. There becomes an agenda for the support of a parent's position on custody and parenting.

The result of this experience for the family is psychological treatment to mend the damage caused by the conflict between the parents. The conflict between the parents is experienced and perceived by the children, and the children are certainly harmed by this parental conflict.

A court will make the ultimate decision on contested issues, which may extend and compound the disharmony between the parties. Cost is extreme as both parties have retained attorneys and possibly paid experts where required for the resolution of the character of property, the value of property, and/or the property division, child custody, parenting, and support.

The goal and desired outcome is driven by win: "give as little as possible, and get as much as possible." Parties are less likely to adhere to the decision of a judge on disputed issues, because the final word on these disputed issues is imposed on the parties!

This model is more likely to produce on-going disputes, a tendency for second-guessing, frustration with the court's orders after a hearing or trial resulting in continued litigation over the property division, custody, visitation, and support, until someone gets it right!

An important by-product of this litigation is how children will experience the stress and conflict created by parents litigating the child custody and visitation issues.

Unfortunately, in this model, children are often used as messengers and spies by their parents when each parent is positioning for their personalized custody and visitation plan.

Extended child custody disputes can require independent therapists for the children and parties.

Finally, in the litigation model, the attorney should make every effort to avoid a contested trial and minimize litigation expenses. The lawyer will need the client's authority to negotiate a settlement with the opposing attorney. No binding agreement should be made without the client's informed consent.

The client may be amenable to mediation of some or all of the outstanding issues in an effort to avoid a contested trial and minimize the litigation expenses.

"Each attorney is under an ethical and professional duty to share and consider Alternative Dispute Resolution possibilities with the client. And, to review and consider the advantages, such as, time and cost savings, greater flexibility for settlement, and often more satisfactory results. Finally, the attorney should suggest a method of dispute resolution to the other side as part of the settlement possibilities." California Practice Guide: Family Law (2009), The Rutter Group, Chapter 1:389.

The Collaboration Approach

"Collaborative law is a way of practicing law whereby attorneys for both of the parties to a dispute agree to assist in resolving conflict by using cooperative strategies rather than adversarial techniques and litigation." The Coalition for Cooperative Divorce (CCD) Workshop, June 2000

The essence of Collaborative law is the shared belief of the Participants, that in typical Family Law matters, it is in the best interest of the parties and their family to commit themselves to avoiding adversarial legal proceedings. There is no court intervention at any stage. The parties choose trained Family Law attorneys, and often other professionals, who may assist them throughout this process to resolve topics and help them make a transition in their lives.

Both parties and their attorneys agree to sign a confidentiality agreement with each other. The purpose of the agreement is to allow for a team approach among the parties and attorneys.

The process may involve different professionals working together in a therapeutic atmosphere to resolve topics established by the parties and their attorney.

The process relies upon a team approach to provide for open communication between the parties. Four-way meetings (collaborative trained attorneys and the parties) are encouraged as a regular process after the initial consultation between the client and collaborative attorney.

Collaborative Law trained lawyers ease the settlement process for the parties.

Team members may be added to the process, and may include the following additional professionals to complete the settlement process:

1. <u>Coaches</u> are persons who assist the parties to develop communication skills, to reduce the stress and strain of the divorce, to support each party to identify goals, to prioritize each party's concerns, and to assist the parties to develop effective communication and co-parenting skills.

2. <u>Child Specialists</u> are persons who meet with the children to assess how the children are doing in the divorce process and to give information to the team that will help to developing an effective co-parenting plan.

3. <u>Financial Consultants</u> are persons who help the parties define their assets and debts, and sources of income. Financial Consultants shall be available to help define the financial goals of the parties and explore the financial options for the future of each party. And, to review the financial options open to the parties to determine their financial well-being for the future.

4. <u>Appraisers and Actuaries</u> are persons who will help the parties determine a value for the division of real estate, a business, a defined pension plan (a plan that provides payments on a monthly basis when the employee reaches a certain age), or defined contribution plans (for example, a 40lk, 403b, 459, profit share, and I.R.A. plans).

All of the specialists work together to make the divorce process as easy as possible.

The parties are able to mutually agree on using the specialist teams to help expedite, resolve, and finalize the divorce process.

The parties pledge in this Agreement to reach a mutual resolution on identified topics without going to court.

Should either party stop the Collaborative Law process, and choose to proceed with any of the disputed topics in court, then the Collaborative attorneys, by the terms of their Agreement, shall not be able to represent their client in court. The parties will need to retain new Family Law counsel to resolve any disputes remaining that will eventually end up in court to be litigated.

The Mediation Approach

In the mediation approach, the parties decide and define the issues to be resolved with an independent party.

The framework in a mediated divorce is "Husband and Wife – Wife and Husband." The so-called "client" is the family. The parties and their children are treated as a unit. The focus is on the present, and restructuring family relations between parents and children, and preserving and improving communication. While it has become certain that the relationship as Husband and Wife is going to be terminated, emphasis is on being Father and Mother forever, and the family finding a way to continue to share each other in a supportive manner.

A mediator's emphasis is on "parents are forever." Parents decide their custody and parenting plan. Anger and hostility are diffused in this approach so that the parties can discuss topics important to them. Hostility is weakened and stress is shortened when the parties work out differences together in a safe setting.

Mediation takes less time and saves money, including taking advantage of positive tax advantages, and avoiding negative tax consequences by mutual agreement. Confidentiality is maintained in this process as statements made in the mediation process are protected, and are not admissible in court. There is no public exposure of the parties in court.

Expectations regarding settlement will be defined and explored together. A fair, equitable, mutually acceptable agreement is the ultimate goal of the parties in this model.

Adherence to the terms of the mediated settlement agreement is more likely, since the terms were created and defined by the parties.

Disagreement and litigation in the future is less likely to occur when the parties have structured the terms of the settlement as opposed to having those terms imposed upon them by the court.

Parents have the opportunity to come together to promote ways to nurture their children and to improve their parenting skills and opportunities.

Parties without children are able to structure their settlement in a safe, creative, inexpensive, and expedited manner.

CHAPTER 3
WHY CHOOSE MEDIATION?

"Becoming involved in a lawsuit is like being ground to bits in a slow mill; it's being roasted at a slow fire; it's being stung to death by single bees; it's being drowned by drops; it's going mad by grains. Hundreds of thousands of people are exposed to torture each year, some of them actually choosing to initiate the process. They invariably find the experience painful, protracted, and expensive. When it has run its course, they often realize that it was futile. Yet there remains a queue of victims impatient for their turn."

Charles Dickens, <u>Bleak House</u>, 1853

"Going to court isn't efficient. It's way too costly, it takes too much time of everyone involved, and it creates stress and discord between people." Judge Duncan said, "If it's discord between just a husband and wife, that happens. But if there are children, that discord spills over to them and that's just not fair." <u>A Judge's Guide to Divorce: Uncommon Advice from the Bench</u>, a book written by Roderic Duncan (retired Alameda County Superior Court, State of California) devoted to explaining that traditional divorce brings out the worst in people, and the result is that the college aspirations of the divorce lawyers' children get supported rather than their client's own kids. Duncan has said, "that litigated divorces can easily cost $100,000 in attorney fees and take more than a year to complete. And, the outcome is rarely as good as when the couples sit down and cooperate."

Lynn Brenner states in her article, "A Saner Smarter Way to Say Goodbye," "More than 40% of American marriages end in divorce, at a whopping average cost of $20,000 to $50,000 per couple in legal fees. But there is a much less expensive way to dissolve a marriage—a mediated divorce. Typical total cost: $4,000 to $5,000."

Mediation enables a couple to raise topics and issues, which are important to them. The mediator contains and manages the parties while they discuss and eventually resolve these topics and issues defined by the parties. The parties are in control of this process and the resolution of the division of community property, community debts, child custody, a parenting plan, and support.

In the mediation encounter, the parties are given the opportunity to fully express their position on the topics defined by them to be resolved.

In this process, the parties are able to express their concerns that might otherwise be dismissed or ignored in the litigation process, controlled by the legal procedure, lawyers, and the lawyer's chosen experts.

Mediation allows for a greater degree of participation by each party in the negotiation and decision-making necessary to reach an agreement.

A mediator will acknowledge and organize each party's personal goals, needs, and interests.

In this forum, the parties are encouraged to explore the reality and possibility for meeting their goals, needs and interests.

The parties are educated as to fundamental family law principles and guidelines so that future decision-making is based upon informed consent.

Each party is provided the opportunity to review options with independent legal counsel, as well as, to review the terms and conditions of any written proposal made between the parties to resolve their conflict.

In the mediation sessions, the parties will have the opportunity to evaluate and reflect on different options for settlement, and then test the reality of each option together in a safe neutral setting.

The sessions with the mediator are private and confidential.

There are no public appearances at a courthouse, as the parties determine the outcome of issues and topics together.

Each party will save time and money by avoiding costly attorney fees and expert fees associated with a contested case.

Stanley L. Bartelmie

Each party is in control of the mediation process. The parties are able to focus on the needs of their children and family, while understanding that the "marital relationship" will be terminated, but the "family relationship" will survive.

The marriage can end with dignity and respect for each other.

The Impact of Divorce Upon Children

Wendy Landes, in her article, "Through the Eyes of Children," provides some clear lessons for family law practitioners and mediators as to the impact of divorce upon children, and these lessons should be considered by divorcing parents as well.

1. Children felt that they were being abandoned when the parenting plan provided for little time with the non-custodial parent.

2. A child may become a caretaker for the parent. This dynamic often causes the child to feel shame and guilt because he/she can never live up to the expectations of being a parent when he/she is a child. Children often take this role into adult life and choose jobs and relationships where they become a caretaker.

3. Children feel as though they are caught in the middle between parents. Children do not have the maturity to cope with the situation. Being put in the middle of conflict often causes them to tell one parent what that parent wants to hear, and the other something else he/she wants to hear. The child cannot be honest with either parent because the child is afraid he/she will be abandoned. This can become a life pattern that must be broken so the child can develop a sense of self that is not driven by fear of abandonment."

4. Children have the ability to manipulate the situation for their own benefit to what they want from their parents, dividing them even further apart in their parenting.

5. Children express fear and even trauma when confronted by the court process in a litigated divorce. Enormous fear, anxiety, and guilt occur if a child is involved in the court process. The child does not want to be abandoned by either parent or take sides.

6. Involving a child in litigation will leave scars that can last a lifetime.

7. Any situation that causes children to act more mature than their age can cause shame and guilt, because children lack the skills to deal with the situation.

It is best when children see that their parents present a cooperative united front. For example, together the parents tell the children about the divorce in a safe setting. The parents will emphasize the importance of their family, even though, Mother and Father will not be living together as Husband and Wife. They will always be a family with Mother and Father taking care of the children.

The children should experience that there will be similar basic rules in each parent's home, such as, bedtime, homework time, and play time. It is important that while the children have experienced that their parents may not see eye to eye in many different ways, but when it comes to a child, the parents present a united front and support each other in decision-making responsibilities. Decisions concerning the child should be joint, unless a medical emergency, and made with information from each parent for the benefit of the child.

The parents can explore working together and defining how they will share their children and avoid the conflict and pain created by a contested custody proceeding.

CHAPTER 4
WHEN IS MEDIATION LIKELY TO SUCCEED?

Mediation involves change. Parties in a dispute typically believe they are right (and most right) about the dispute. Each party may or may not understand their own interests and those of the other party, and each may have unrealistic expectations. Each party may be unwilling to treat the other with any degree of respect. It takes time to address these issues, and it takes time for the people to change their minds. It is important for parties in a mediation to allow for these changes to occur.

Kendall C. Reed,

"The Art of Mediation:

Ten Rules for Effective Participation."

Mediation works well when the parties are willing to come together in a safe setting and listen to each other.

There has to be mutual consideration and respect for the dignity of the mediation process. This process works well with couples who can manage their emotions.

When the parties have multiple issues to resolve, then mediation is a meaningful option. If the parties wish to be in control of the process and the outcome, then mediation is a good choice.

When the conflict between the parties includes communication, the process of mediation with simple rules for communication monitored by a mediator can be an effective way to help couples talk through and resolve their disputes.

Mediation is successful when couples are willing to work together with a professional who will help them bring about an end to their marriage.

If the parties have a relationship or had a relationship in the past, which can be a foundation for following ground rules, listening to each other, and reaching agreement on disputed topics, then mediation is a good choice for the parties.

When the parties want to save time, money and the grinding stress associated with litigating their divorce, then mediation is a positive choice.

A resolution of the issues is possible without one party wanting or insisting on assigning fault or liability to the other party.

Personal and emotional issues exist, which can be expressed, as opposed to repressed, in a safe setting with mutual respect for honoring the ground rules established for the mediation process.

The parties perceive the facts differently, and in the mediation process they are able to confront the differences of position/opinion on each topic in a safe setting.

When there are multiple topics to resolve, then mediation is a powerful and effective model for the parties to explore the creative possibilities for settlement.

<u>Suggestions For Better Communication</u>

The parties will need to have the ability to follow basic ground rules and be aware of these concepts:

1. It is imperative that the parties use "I" messages instead of "you" or "we" messages when communicating about each other. The parties should begin their sentences with I instead of you or we.

2. The mediation session is not to be used as a format to verbally assault the other party, and using "I" messages will help avoid this temptation.

3. Each party is open to express their ideas and goals in a safe setting without interruption.

4. When the parties find it difficult to directly communicate with each other, and emotions build and get in the way of the conversation, then the mediator should become the focus of the direction of communication from each party. A sign that the parties are unable to check their emotions and listen to the other party occurs when one or both of the parties is interrupting the other party when they are speaking, and they interrupting party cannot help it.

5. The time for communicating ideas and goals with the mediator should be substantially the same for each party.

Sharon Ellison, M.S. in her article, "Powerful Non-Defensive Communication" indicates that when a person asks questions, makes statements, and predicts consequences in an open sincere way without trying to control how other people respond, then people are more likely to respect us, and we can strengthen personal and professional relationships.

1. <u>Ask Questions</u>: In order to gather thorough information to understand accurately what the person means, believes, or feels.

   However, avoid using a question to express your own opinion or to entrap others.

2. <u>Make Statements</u>:

   a) About what you hear the other person saying;

   b) Any contradictions you perceive in the person's tone of voice, body language, and words;

   c) About your conclusions regarding the person's overt and covert messages; and,

   d) About your own reactions, your feelings, your beliefs, and your reasoning.

Example: If the speaker continues to act irritable and denies it when asked, saying harshly, "I'm Fine" You might respond with a four part statement:

"When I hear you saying that you are in a good mood and at the same time I see that your are rolling your eyes and shrugging your shoulders, then I believe something is wrong, but you do not want to tell me, and so I feel frustrated and not sure if I should ask you more questions or leave you alone."

e) <u>Hear</u>: When I hear you saying that you are in a good mood . . .

f) <u>See</u>: . . . and at the same time I see that you are rolling your eyes and shrugging your shoulders

g) <u>Conclude</u>: . . . then I believe that something is wrong but you do not want to tell me

h) <u>Reaction</u>: . . . and so I feel frustrated and am not sure if I should ask you more questions or leave you alone.

Tips For Productive Dialog

Susan Allison, <u>Conscious Divorce</u> (2001), has provided some communication tips for productive dialogue with parties during stressful times:

1. Agree on a time and a neutral place convenient for both parties to have a talk.

2. Agree on the amount of time you need, and do not exceed that time limit unless there is mutual agreement to do so.

3. Take turns speaking and allow equal time for each party.

4. When you listen, have focused attention and do not interrupt the other party.

5. Breathe deeply when you are hearing things being said that are difficult to hear.

6. Sometimes it is good to summarize what you have heard to be sure you understand. This helps the other person feel that their point of view has been heard.

7. Avoid the "you or we messages"—You always . . . ." It can make the other person defensive, and might lead to escalation of tension, frustration and anger.

8. Use "I messages" to clearly state what is going on with you. A formula: I feel . . . (admit your honest feelings) when you . . . (give a specific thing). I'd like you to . . . (do something) . . . because . . . (give your reasons). The key point is to communicate clearly what is happening for you and why, and what you are needing and why. This helps to develop understanding and compassion.

9. Pay attention to the amount of time you spend, and respect each other's time and space.

10. Congratulate yourself for being aware that communication is important, useful, and challenging.

Diane C. Shearer, M.A., CFLE, has written an article, "Five Critical Questions Divorce Mediators Should Ask," in which she says:

"I began to ask a few simple questions that were helpful in facilitating a real shift in how parents think about their future interactions with each other. After all, if we aspire to peaceful customized agreements, we need to find out what the customs of the family are."

(1) How have you typically handled conflict as a couple?

Will help the parties to frame a parenting plan that reduces the conflict the children might otherwise experience.

(2) What issues caused conflict in the marriage?

Will help the parties and mediator frame the parenting plan to avoid conflict and create as many uniform situations in each home (bedtime, homework time, same chores) to demonstrate to the children that the parents are working together for their benefit.

(3) What will you do when a conflict comes up that is not addressed in the parenting plan? Decisions in connection with the health care, education, religion, and activities of the children will need to be made by the parents and each parent should help develop a communication protocol to confront these situations as a precaution to preventing confusion or even conflict about decisions to be made for the children's benefit.

(4) How have you kept your children connected to their extended family members?

It is imperative that parents put together a parenting plan that will help preserve family ties.

(5) How is this healthy, enforceable or realistic?

When parents wish to provide wording in their Agreement that is self-focused instead of child focused, then the parties should consider these topics to get better focused on healthy and productive terms and conditions for their Agreement.

CHAPTER 5

WHEN IS MEDIATION LIKELY TO FAIL?

When one of the parties is seriously incapacitated at the time of the mediation. For example, if one party is a drug or alcohol abuser. If a party is suffering from a mental illness, has an age limitation, has an extremely low self-interest or low self-esteem to such an extent as to interfere with their ability to define and assert one's needs, interests, and goals for the mediation process.

When one party is too fearful or emotional to represent his or her interests in the mediation process.

When a party is seeking a definite result on a central issue and/or a party is stuck on a central issue and needs vindication to be satisfied about the final result on a central issue. For example, one party has a defined plan for sharing the children with no interest for the in-put of the other parent in developing a parenting plan together. One parent believes they know what is best for the children, and is not willing to be flexible about sharing the children. Or, when other family members have put extreme pressure on a parent to implement a defined parenting plan with no regard for the other parent's position, or what might be in the best interest of the children.

If a party has a preconceived notion regarding the division of property, parenting, and/or support issues, and is not willing to change position in the mediation process.

If a party will only be satisfied when the other party suffers financially.

One of the parties refuses to participate in the mediation process in good faith.

When distrust between the parties is so severe that the parties have no belief that a mutual agreement will ever be accomplished, and there is no interest in the prospect of resolving their issues together.

Franklin R. Garfied is a family lawyer and mediator in Los Angeles, California. He indicates that there are three primary reasons why the mediation may fail:

1. The parties feel pressured to make decisions based upon incomplete or incorrect information.

    Therefore, It is fundamental, in the mediation process, that the parties shall have the information needed to make informed decisions. This information may be exchanged between the parties, and the parties may need to retain an independent third party to provide the information needed to make an informed decision in the mediation process.

2. The parties have unrealistic expectations that contaminate the decision-making process,

    The mediator and other third party neutrals will have a duty to be agents of reality for the parties . . . (For example, a Wife who believes that the spousal support amount is solely controlled by the marital standard of living when the income available for support may be the controlling factor. Or, a Husband who believes that his Wife will need to get a job immediately when she has been a homemaker and not held a job in more than 10 years, and that an option might be to acquire education and/or training in a vocation to prepare for employment.

3. The parties are unable to put aside their feelings, or at least to understand that their feelings are mostly irrelevant to the legal and financial issues involved in a marital breakup.

    This becomes obvious in court where the parties' feelings do not constitute admissible evidence. In mediation, the parties are free to express their feelings, and will keep their feelings in check so that topics defined can be resolved, and to avoid "dumping" on a party. A good technique for the parties to use in mediation when speaking to each other is to start any sentence with "I" instead of "you" or "we." The parties are dealing with sadness, anger, resentment and fear. Divorcing couples tend to have empathy for sadness, but this does not carry over to anger, resentment and fear.

CHAPTER 6
CHOOSING A MEDIATOR

"Mediation is a conflict resolution process in which one or more impartial persons intervene in a conflict with the disputants' consent and help them negotiate a mutually acceptable agreement. The mediator does not take sides or decide how the dispute should be resolved" Alaska Judicial Council, "A Consumer Guide to Selecting a Mediator"

At this time there is no certification process for mediators in California. The Rules of Court define how mediators should conduct their practice. You will need to inquire about the reputation of the mediators in your community by calling family law lawyers for a reference, and checking the local Superior Court panel of approved mediators. Reviewing internet web sites for background information on mediators, and interviewing the mediator you have chosen is also suggested.

The current recommended standards for mediators on California Superior Court panels are as follows:

1. 40 hours of training within the past two years from a recognized and approved provider.

2. 32 hours of training from one approved provider, which covers 8 hours of conflict resolution, ethics, confidentiality, role play, rules of court, culture & gender issues, and the role of the mediator in drafting a mediated Agreement.

3. 4 hours of Continuing Legal Education every 3 years to include 1 hour of ethics, 1 hour regarding self-represented litigants, and 2 hours of general education.

Some Questions for the Mediator

David Grappo, a retired Oakland attorney who often represented parties in mediation has posed eleven questions to ask a potential mediator in his article entitled, "Active Process." I have extracted some of the relevant questions applicable to family law mediators in a divorce setting.

First, How do you see mediation as different from other types of dispute resolution?

Many persons call themselves mediators and actually they are providing a service as an early neutral evaluator, settlement conference officer, or even arbiter. Be sure to find a skilled neutral mediator. A person trained to act as an independent neutral guiding the mediation process.

Second, What is your view of the mediator's role in mediation?

A mediator remains neutral and independent throughout the process. When the negotiations stall or hostility occurs between the parties, will there be an expectation that the mediator will be assertive and involved in the negotiation process. Mediators possess skills to guide parties through hostility and/or being grounded on a position.

Third, What mediation training did you have?

How was the mediator trained? And, how does the mediator conduct the mediation process?

Fourth, Describe your experience as a mediator.

While the process of mediation may be familiar to the mediator, the subject area of the case may be unfamiliar to the mediator. Many professional mediators are attorneys, and the process may be more important than the knowledge of the substantive law, which attorney- mediators are likely to possess. Many attorney mediators may have represented clients in divorce court over many years before limiting their practice to mediation or a combination of each process.

To acquire an understanding of the mediation process, the Alaska Judicial Council provides "A Consumer Guide to Selecting a Mediator" and the "Five Steps to Choosing a Mediator."

1. Decide What you Want from Mediation

   Are you looking for a directed mediation with options presented to you, or are you looking for a mediator who will resist providing options so that you can be responsible for the outcome? Look at your strengths and weaknesses as a negotiator and look at those characteristics for your spouse. Both parties need to be able to freely communicate in the mediation process. A hallmark of the mediation process is that the parties are able to speak about their goals and interests even though these are not fully attained in the agreement reached between the parties.

2. Get a List of Mediators

   Ask a friend, therapist, or another professional for a referral. Look on the internet; get names from a family law mediation panel with the local bar association; and, use the yellow pages.

3. Look over Mediator's Written Qualifications

Review the mediator's training and promotional material. Evaluate the mediator's experience, such as, number of mediations conducted.

4. Interview Mediators

Good qualities include neutrality, emotional stability and maturity, integrity, and sensitivity. How has your training and experience prepared you to help us work out this specific dispute?

5. Evaluate information and Make a Decision

Does the mediator display skills to gather background information; communicate with the parties and help the parties communicate; refer the parties to other people or programs where appropriate; analyze information; help the parties agree; and, manage and document information?

CHAPTER 7

WHAT OBLIGATIONS DOES THE MEDIATOR OWE TO THE PARTIES?

Attorneys acting as neutral mediators are not "legal counsel" for either party. However, an attorney accepting the role of neutral mediator has the same duty of full disclosure as an attorney accepting the representation of clients with actual or potentially conflicting interests. Neutral attorney mediators are in a position to influence the conflicting positions taken by the parties to the mediation. Attorney mediators must fully disclose any facts that might cause either party to believe they will not be impartial. There should be no undisclosed "side understandings" with either party.

The mediation process is treated like a settlement discussion. The court system and public policy encourages settlements between parties, and protects the settlement process and mediation communications from being admitted at trial to allow the parties to speak freely in an effort to settle their disputes.

The following are excerpts from the California Rules of Court.

Explanation of the Mediation Process

At or before the outset of the mediation, the mediator must provide all participants with a general explanation of:

(1) The nature of the mediation process;

(2) The procedures to be used; and

(3) The role of the mediator, the parties, and the other possible participants, such as, a joint expert to define the value of an asset to be divided between the parties, or a family therapist to help the parties establish healthy communication patterns and to develop a parenting plan together.

Procedural Fairness

The mediation process must be conducted in a procedurally fair manner. This means a balanced process in which each party is given an opportunity to participate and make decisions without undue influence. The parties are given substantially equal time to express their concerns in a safe setting.

Ground rules are established to prevent name calling and abusive language. There should be an emphasis on "I" messages over "You" messages when the parties are beginning a sentence in their communication with each other. For example,

"You never paid attention to the credit card charges." Instead, "I have been frustrated with the lack of attention to the credit card charges for a long time." What is initially a personal attack becomes an acceptable statement that the parties can begin to look upon and understand.

However, it is important to note that a mediator is not obligated to ensure the substantive fairness of an agreement reached by the parties. The parties are free to divide their community property in a manner that they choose, which may include an equal or unequal division of the community property.

Confidentiality

At the outset of the first mediation session, the mediator must provide the participants with a general explanation of the confidentiality of the mediation proceedings.

A mediator must not use information that is acquired in confidence in the course of a mediation outside the mediation for personal gain.

The mediator and the parties will communicate as a team. The mediator will not communicate with one party, unless the other party is present. When using the internet for communication, the mediator and parties will all be addressed together on the emails. If there is a good reason to use the telephone, then there will be a conference call, so that all parties are present for the communication on the telephone.

Diligence

A mediator must allow the mediation to progress in a timely manner. If a mediation session is scheduled, then the mediator must keep that time period free of any other commitments.

Impartiality

A mediator must maintain impartiality toward the parties in the mediation process at all times.

Representation and other Professional Services

A mediator must inform the parties, at the outset of the first mediation session, that during the mediation he or she will not represent either party as a lawyer or perform professional services in any capacity other than as an impartial mediator.

Subject to the principles of impartiality and self-determination, a mediator may provide information or opinions that he or she is qualified by training or experience to provide. Many family law mediators are or had been practicing family law lawyers. It is very important for the participants to remember that the family law mediator is not acting as a lawyer for either party at any time in the mediation process. It would be unethical for a lawyer to represent the parties when they have such diverse interests competing at the same time.

The attorney mediator may provide information to parties regarding current legal principles to allow the parties to have information available to them to be informed when making independent decisions. The parties should be given sufficient time to review their mediated settlement agreement with independent family law counsel.

At any time in the mediation process, if a party wishes, he/she would be free to "check-in" with independent family law counsel.

Recommending Other Services

A mediator may recommend the use of other services in connection with the mediation process. The mediator must disclose any related personal or financial interests if recommending the services of a specific individual or organization. For example, when the parties need to use an appraiser, real estate agent, or certified public accountant to obtain a value for an asset or to determine income for support, because they are unable to reach an agreement as to value or income, it may become necessary to use these outside services to provide the information needed to help the parties reach agreement.

The Interests of Non-participants

Mediators may bring to the attention of the parties interests of others affected by the agreement to be made by the parties in mediation.

For example, if the parties co-own property or a business with third parties.

Settlement Agreements

A mediator may present possible settlement options and terms for discussion. A mediator may also assist the parties in preparing a written settlement agreement, provided that in doing so, the mediator confines their assistance to stating the settlement as determined by the parties.

Discretionary Termination and Withdrawal

A mediator may suspend or terminate the mediation process or withdraw as mediator when he or she reasonably believes the circumstances require it, including when he or she suspects that:

(1) The mediation is being used to further illegal conduct;

(2) A party is unable to participate meaningfully in negotiations; or

(3) Continuation of the process would cause significant harm to either party, or a third party.

Manner of Withdrawal

The mediator must withdraw from the mediation process without violating the obligation of confidentiality and in a manner that will cause the least possible harm to either party.

Truthfulness

A mediator must be truthful and accurate in marketing his or her mediation services. Further, a mediator may indicate that he or she is a member of a particular court's panel or list of approved mediators. But, unless specifically permitted by the court, the mediator must not indicate that he or she is approved, endorsed, certified, or licensed by the court.

In marketing his or her mediation services, a mediator must not:

(1) Promise or guarantee results; or

(2) Make any statement that directly or indirectly implies bias in favor of one party over another.

Solicitation of Business

A mediator must not solicit business from a party in a mediation proceeding while that mediation is pending.

Compensation and Gift

A mediator must comply with any applicable requirements concerning compensation established by statute or the court.

No contingency fee: The amount or nature of a mediator's fee must not be made contingent upon the outcome of the mediation.

At the outset of the mediation, the mediator must disclose to the parties in writing any fees, costs, or charges to be paid to the mediator by the parties. A mediator must abide by any agreement that is reached concerning compensation.

A mediator must not at any time solicit or accept from or give any participant or affiliate of a participant any gift, bequest, or favor that might reasonably raise a question concerning the mediator's impartiality.

Complaint Procedure

The court may reprimand a mediator, remove a mediator from the court's panel or list, or otherwise prohibit a mediator from receiving future mediation referrals from the court, if the mediator fails to comply with the rules of conduct for mediators, when applicable.

CHAPTER 8

THE IMPORTANCE OF DETERMINING THE DATE OF SEPARATION

The date of separation is legally important and represents the date that one party communicated, by language and conduct, a clear intention to terminate the marriage.

Here are examples of behaviors that support the concept of legal separation:

1) The most obvious act is when one party prepares and files a Petition for Dissolution of the Marriage with the court.

2) One party permanently moves out of the family residence.

3) The parties begin to divide and close joint accounts, and open separate accounts.

4) Family and friends are openly advised that the marital relationship will be terminated.

5) All sexual relations with the other spouse are terminated.

6) The parties do not take vacations together.

7) No further marriage counseling occurs with the spouse.

8) One party does not recognize the spouse's birthday, anniversary, and holidays by sending cards and/or presents.

9) The spouse moving out of the residence does not return regularly for meals, to do laundry, or to do maintenance.

10) The parties divide payments for common bills.

11. If residing in the same residence, then they do not share the same bedroom, meals, groceries, phone number, and one party may open a PO Box number in their sole name and use it as a return address.

12. There is a termination of the current estate plan and creation of a new estate plan.

The following behaviors would tend to support an on-going marital relationship:

1) Don't move out of the family residence.

2) Don't file an action for legal separation or dissolution of marriage with the court, and discourage your spouse from doing this.

3) Continue sexual relations with your spouse.

4) Insist on continuing the use of joint bank accounts.

5) Request and engage in marital counseling.

6) Take a vacation together.

7) Do the other spouse's laundry.

8) Maintain joint credit card accounts.

9) Continue using the same phone numbers.

10) Continue to socialize together with mutual friends.

11) Recognize special events, such as, birthdays, anniversary, and holidays by giving each other cards and presents.

12) Attend children's school and sports activities together.

13) Refuse to recognize that the marriage is over.

The date of separation, under family law principles, defines when certain property, such as, retirement plans, the valuation of a self- employed business, accrued vacation, compensation time, accrued sick leave, stock, and stock option plans, 401k Account, I.R.A, 403b, 457 Plans, and other income tax deferred accounts are valued by the court. This may include a division of any dividends, interest, losses and gains realized in these assets, from the date of separation until the actual date of division between the parties. In mediation, the parties have the ability to define the date that their assets are valued and divided.

Each party's income will become separate property on the date of separation, and so will any and all contributions after the date of separation made to tax deferred savings plans, defined pension plans, stock acquisition plans, stock option grants, bonus payments, commissions, and accrued vacation and sick leave plans. In mediation, the parties are able to treat income differently to meet their needs.

The date of separation under California law defines the term for the marriage as a period of time between the date of marriage to the date of separation. And, 10-year marriages or longer are deemed long-term marriages under California law.

Whereas, under Federal law, the term of the marriage is defined as the period of time between the date of marriage, until the date of marriage status termination. A marriage of 10 years or more under Federal law will afford enhanced or derivative Social Security benefits and other benefits related to a spouse employed by the federal government or U.S. military, and not otherwise available to couples married less than 10 years. A couple can plan the termination date of the marital status to insure the 10 years duration to protect social security and other military benefits, even though, they are legally separated prior to a 10 years period.

CHAPTER 9

GENERAL LEGAL CONCEPTS FOR PROPERTY DIVISION

<u>**Separate or Community Property?**</u>

The family law court is bound by codes and case law, which provide precedent for determining how to characterize, divide and value community property, determine custody and parenting plans, as well as determine the amount of child and spousal support.

Parties in mediation are not controlled by statutes and case law like a judge ruling in the family court.

The parties can value and divide their community property in a substantially equal manner, or unequally, if they choose. The important factor for each party is to completely understand the character and fair market value of their property before considering proposals to divide the property.

Each party will become informed about their assets and debts in the exercise of completing a Schedule of Assets and Debts, which the parties prepare independently and exchange with each other.

The Schedule of Assets and Debts will provide a <u>full</u> disclosure of all assets and debts owned by the parties, whether community property, separate property, or a mixture of community and separate property. This is a prerequisite in California to the parties signing an Agreement to divide their assets and debts.

Property acquired during a marriage can take on many forms like the following items:

1. Improved real estate

2. Barren land

3. Time share Investments

4. Leasehold interests

5. Lease deposits

6. Promissory Notes

7. Frequent Flyer Airline Miles

8. Country Club and Fitness Club Memberships

9. Season tickets

10. Reward programs

11. Animals

12. Vehicles

13. Boats and trailers

14. Life insurance (cash value and security for support)

15. Term life insurance (insurability of a spouse and security for support?)

16. Furniture, Furnishings and Appliances

17. Wine-Stamp-Coin-Baseball Card-Sport Memorabilia-Lladro and other Collectibles

18. Employee benefits

19. Stock, Stock Purchase Plans, Stock Option and Restricted Stock Unit Plans

20. Bonds, Treasury Bills, and Certificates of Deposit

21. Bank accounts, Brokerage accounts, and Tax deferred accounts

22. Personal injury and Workers compensation awards

23. A Sole Proprietorship, Corporation, Partnership, Limited Partnership, and other business interests

24. Copyrights and royalties

Three Concepts for Dividing Property

When considering the division of property acquired during the Marriage, it will be important for each spouse to understand three concepts:

First, what is the **"character"** of the property. Is the property "separate" or "community" (quasi-community")?

Second, what is the **"value"** of the property being divided?

Third, how will the parties determine the **"division"** of their property?

How will the parties determine the Character of their property?

In California there are three (3) types of property:

Community, Quasi-community and Separate.

Community property is generally all property acquired during the marriage. Exceptions to this general rule include gifts and inheritances received during the marriage.

Each spouse has a one-half ownership interest in the community property.

Quasi-community property is property acquired outside the

State of California while the parties are married and residing in California. An example of quasi-community property would be a condominium purchased in the state of Nevada, while the parties are married and living in California. Quasi-community property is treated like community property, and each spouse has an undivided one-half interest in these assets.

Separate property is generally property that a spouse owned prior to the marriage, or acquired during the marriage by inheritance or by gift.

On and after the "date of separation," each party's effort, skill and labor become the separate property of each party.

Income earned after the date of separation, including contributions to tax deferred savings plans, and other retirement, stock and pension plans is generally the separate property of the earner.

And, other accumulations directly acquired using income earned after the date of separation is generally the separate property of the earning party.

Today, each party is required to fill-in and identify all known assets and debts in a Declaration of Disclosure. This Declaration includes, at a minimum, A Schedule of Assets and Debts as well as an Income and Expense Declaration. In California, the careful preparation and exchange of a Declaration of Disclosure is a requirement before the parties can sign an Agreement to divide their assets and debts, and resolve any permanent support issues.

This exercise educates each party as to the extent of their community property, quasi-community property, and their separate property, and prepares them to speak about options for the division of their property.

How will the parties Value their property?

Parties in mediation may agree on a value of their property based on their personal knowledge, and by mutual agreement.

When the parties have a defined benefit retirement plan or pension plan, commercial property, stock options, valuable collectibles, valuable art, and jewelry, then the parties may wish to retain a joint expert to define the value of their property.

The parties can use resources at their disposal, like Kelly Blue

Book, recent sales of similar property, advertising announcements in the newspaper, magazines, or by using the World Wide Web. For example, Zillow.com for real estate information, Craig's List for real estate and personal property. A combination of these resources can be very helpful.

How will the parties divide their property?

Generally, the parties will usually divide their community assets and debts by agreement, and be awarded their own separate assets and debts as their sole and separate property. However, the parties in a mediation setting are free to determine what is in their best interest considering all factors, including the decision for support, and the parenting plan created for sharing the children.

Parties in mediation may divide their community and even their separate property in any manner they choose, or exchange property in any manner they choose, and be as creative as they wish in dividing their assets and debts, including owning property as tenants in common after the termination of their marital status.

It is important that the parties understand the nature and character of their property when dividing, exchanging, or jointly owning their property after their marriage is terminated.

It is this informed basis, which provides each party with the ability to do as they wish with their assets and debts.

Generally, by law, the court must divide the community property assets and community property debts equally between the parties, and assign each party their separate property assets and separate property debts.

The parties in a mediation setting can divide their community property and assign their separate property in any manner they choose when they have:

1) Made a complete disclosure of their assets and debts
2) Defined the character of the assets and debts
3) Defined the value of their property
4) Defined the extent of their obligations
5) Reviewed any reimbursement claims in connection with the acquisition or improvement of property
6. Understood the legal consequences of their decisions

When considering any property item, the couple will decide the character of the property, the value of the property, and the division of the property.

Some different methods of dividing assets and debts include:

In-Kind division: This is where the parties each take one-half of the asset or debt, such as, bank accounts, credit card debts, and stock shares.

Trade-off division: The parties agree to pick and choose certain items of property. For example, one party chooses the joint savings account and the other party chooses the family automobile.

Piece of Cake division: Is very useful in short-term marriages where there has been a small accumulation of community property, or for dividing furniture, furnishings, appliances, and tools, which have lost their fair market value, but have a sentimental value to the parties. One party makes two lists of property which are of substantially equal value, and the other party is allowed to choose one of the lists of property, and the other party (list maker) receives the other list of items.

One party values the property and the other party chooses the property division: The party choosing the property valued by the other party may choose up to one-half of the value of the community property. Or, alternatively, the choosing party may not choose to pick up to one-half the value of the property, and then those items remaining are to the valuing party by default. The parties can decide on whether to have an equalizer payment from the party receiving greater value of property to the other party to substantially equalize the value of the property divided between the parties.

You take it or I will take it division: One party values an asset for the other party to take. And, if the other party refuses, then the party valuing the asset receives the asset at the same value.

Appraisal and alternate selection: An appraiser is selected by the mutual agreement of the parties to value items in question, then the parties choose items alternately. The party to choose first is determined by a flip of a coin. The values of items chosen by each party can be totally valued, and if not substantially equal, then the party receiving the greater value shall reimburse the other party to equalize the value of the personal property divided.

Sale or Donation to Charity: The parties agree on the sale of certain items at a public sale or to a private party with the proceeds of sale divided between the parties, or used as an off-set to equalize the division of assets and debts between the parties.

Some parties may agree to donate and divide the charitable deduction on their income tax returns.

Sealed Bid: When the parties are not able to agree on the value of certain identified items, then they each submit a sealed bid for the identified items. The bids are opened simultaneously, and the one bidding the higher amount will get the asset. An equalizer payment can be calculated to correct the disparity in value when the division under sealed bid is not substantially equal. This can be very useful when the parties have operated a family business together and each party would like to own the business, family residence, or other identified asset.

Auction: The parties bid against each other with an agreed minimum incremental increase for each over bid. The highest bid gets the asset with an equalizer payment due to the other party, if necessary, after considering the value of division of all the community assets and debts. When the parties are auctioning their family residence or business, it is appropriate that each party have an advisor present.

These methods of dividing property also resolve the issue of value and can be utilized by the parties and considered in mediation where appropriate.

However, the parties can divide their property in-kind where each party takes one-half of the asset.

The parties can elect to continue to own property together as tenants-in-common for a specified time with conditions for sale and division, or buy-out of the other spouse's interest in the asset in the future.

The parties can assign specified assets and debts to each other in a trade-off approach.

CHAPTER 10

REAL ESTATE

Real Estate and Different Ways to Divide the Family Residence

Real property is land. Real property may include anything growing on it, attached to it, or erected on it. Land and its improvements usually means a family residence.

The parties can sell, trade, off-set, buy-out, or continue to own this realty as tenants in common.

One option for couples with children who wish to continue to own the family residence is a plan where the parents alternate living in the home on an alternating weekly basis, or other defined basis. This is commonly called "bird nesting."

Or, one spouse may retain the exclusive possession of the family residence.

Both of these approaches keep the children in their familiar home, neighborhood and schools.

The parties can agree on one spouse having exclusive, use, possession and control of the family residence subject to the terms of an agreement to continue to own the family residence as tenants in common.

Deferring the Sale of the Family Residence

Drastic economic circumstances in the real estate and job markets have created an inherent interest in deferring the sale of the family residence.

Divorcing parties, especially with minor children, are considering a delay in the division of the family residence as an important option for the division of the family residence.

Children are able to remain in the same home, neighborhood, schools and church, and are impacted by the divorce less severely than if they are uprooted from these familiar attachments.

Couples are looking at retaining ownership of their family residence, so that it can hopefully be sold for a profit in the future, and to stabilize the lives of their children.

The parties are considering negotiating a reduction in the amount of the mortgage balance and monthly payment with the bank to reflect the fair market value of the residence, and to avoid a foreclosure proceeding.

One of the parties may need time to acquire the ability to purchase the other party's community interest in the home, and the parties agree to make an arrangement to accomplish this goal, and to avoid the costs of a listed sale, to eliminate a capital gains tax, and to allow one party to continue to be a real estate owner when it may otherwise be problematic for that party to qualify to purchase a new residence.

The character of the family home, which qualifies for application of a deferred sale of the home can be a community property asset, mixed asset, or even the separate property of the non-resident or out-spouse (party living out of the family home), who is the child support obligor. Allowing the spouse and children to remain in the family residence can be a form of child support beneficial to the parties and the children.

When the parties consider a deferred sale of their home, they must determine whether it is economically feasible to do so:

(1) Will the house payments (mortgage, property taxes, and insurance) during the deferred sale period be manageable?

(2) Is the resident spouse (in-spouse) able to maintain and preserve the condition of the home comparable to the time when the in-spouse took exclusive possession of the home subject to normal wear and tear?

An "economic feasibility" determination by the parties shall include review of the following aspects in connection with a deferred division of the family residence:

First, the length of time the child(ren) has resided in the home.

Second, the child's placement or grade in school, and how much longer would the child(ren) be likely to attend a neighborhood school.

Third, the accessibility and convenience of the home to the child's school, other facilities used by the child and available to the child, including child-care.

Fourth, whether the home has been adapted or modified to accommodate any physical disabilities of a child or a resident parent in a manner such that a change in residence may adversely affect the ability of the resident parent to meet those special needs.

Fifth, the emotional detriment to the child associated with a change in residence.

Sixth, the extent to which the location of the family residence permits the resident parent to continue his or her employment.

Seventh, the financial ability of each parent to obtain suitable housing should the family residence be immediately sold and the proceeds divided.

Eighth, determining the tax consequences to the parties, and the requirement for a reservation of jurisdiction for the maintenance of the home and tax consequences.

Ninth, determining the economic detriment to the nonresident parent in the event of a deferred sale of home order. A deferred sale might interfere both with the out-spouse's ability to acquire suitable housing for "frequent and continuing" contact with the children.

For example, the out-spouse's separate property interest in the home may be a just and equitable factor to consider in deferring the owner's occupancy/sale of the home or in limiting the term for the deferred occupancy/sale.

The Agreement deferring the sale of the family home must specify its duration.

The deferral of the sale of the family residence may be an independent integral part of the division of the community property.

When the parties agree to a deferred division of their family residence, they should review and consider the following:

1. **<u>Record a new Deed</u>** identifying each spouse as a Tenant in Common as to an undivided one-half interest each. There are two very important reasons to convert the title to Tenancy in Common: (1) This form of title allows for each party to include and dispose of their community property share of the asset as they wish in their estate planning, and (2) it protects each party's undivided one-half ownership interest from becoming an asset of the bankruptcy estate under the jurisdiction of the bankruptcy court should one of the parties file for protection from creditors in a bankruptcy proceeding during the joint ownership.

2. Provide for the **<u>exclusive use, possession and control of the f<u>amily residence</u></u>** by one of the spouses. The party who is living permanently in the home is the

in-spouse or resident spouse. The other party is the out-spouse and may retain the right to come to the residence for parenting duties, maintenance or repairs on the property, all subject to advance notice to come to the residence, unless to implement the defined parenting plan. The parties may mutually agree on how to share the possession of the residence, including keeping the possession exclusive to the resident spouse. Or, the spouses can choose to alternate exclusive possession of the family residence defining their shared exclusive possession. For example, the parents alternate one-week intervals in the home. This has been referred to loosely as "bird nesting."

Under current tax law, the out-spouse can continue to consider the deferral of $250,000 of gain on the family residence so long as this residence continues to be the primary residence for the out-spouse, and in spite of the exclusive possession of the family residence by the in-spouse. For purposes of the IRS Section 121 exclusion, the out-spouse is treated as using the property as his or her principal residence during any period of ownership that the other spouse is granted use of the property under a divorce or separation instrument. IRC Section 121(d)(3)(B)

3. The parties shall **determine support** and the obligation to maintain the principal, interest, taxes and insurance connected to the family residence. This arrangement can create a mutual tax advantageous situation, whereby the in-spouse pays the mortgage and taxes, and the out-spouse pays family support to resident spouse. The in-spouse must include the family support as income for the annual income

tax return, and the out-spouse deducts the payments from gross income for the annual income tax return. The in-spouse will write-off the deductible interest and real estate taxes from the family support received to reduce the total amount of income on the annual income tax return. The parties may review this approach with a C.P.A. to maximize the mutual income tax benefit of using family support. Family support is unallocated combined spousal and child support, and is fully deductible provided that it meets all of the requirements for spousal support deductibility. The obligation to pay family support must terminate on the supported spouse's death. IRC Section 71(b)(1)(D) No part of the family support payment can be fixed as child support, or reduced or terminated on a contingency related to a child. IRC Section 71(C)(1) and IRC Section 71(c)(2) (A). Or, the parties can use a more traditional Guideline approach to support, and make any mutually agreed adjustments for the principal, interest, taxes and insurance, which will mutually benefit the parties.

4. The parties should compare and contrast the monthly **fair rental value of the home against the monthly cost of the loan principal, loan interest, taxes and insurance (PITI) amount.** If the PITI payments are greater than the fair rental value, then consider options for sharing these expenses. For example, the out-spouse may make the tax payment and write-off this expense on the annual income tax return, or share a percentage of all the expenses, and take the appropriate expense for income taxes where appropriate. The amount equal to one-half of the difference between the monthly Fair Rental Value and the PITI

could be deducted from the support each month or deferred and reimbursed out of escrow on sale, or as a credit for the buy-out formula. The parties may meet with a C.P.A. to find the best tax appropriate assignment of these payments with a consideration for the use of family support, assigning dependents, and other support options. Or, the in-spouse may delay a monthly reimbursement to compensate for the monthly overpayment of the PITI compared to the monthly fair rental value to be paid out of escrow on the sale of the family residence, or as part of the buy-out formula instead of a listed sale.

If the monthly fair rental value is greater than the monthly PITI payment, then the amount equal to one-half of the difference (or any other agreed amount) could be added to support or deferred and reimbursed out of escrow on sale or as part of the calculation for a buy-out formula, or as a deduction to the monthly support.

Whether to grant a net fair rental value offset against child support lies within the discretion of the parties.

5. **<u>Define the term of the tenancy in common?</u>** The parties may have a "look and see" approach for the rapidly changing value of the real estate market during the joint ownership. The parents may consider continuity and consistency for the children based on their ages; or to allow a child to complete their education at the same school; and to allow a child to complete an activity in the neighborhood. The parties may agree to provide additional time to allow one party to develop the ability to pay for the other party's community interest in the home in a "buy-

out" arrangement for division of the family residence. They may need the time to provide for the opportunity to negotiate with the bank to define and work out a new loan, which more accurately reflects the current market value of the home in lieu of a foreclosure action. When one of the parties would not be able to qualify to buy a home on the open market, but would be able to purchase the other party's interest in the family residence in a reasonably short period of time, and thereby become a home owner by arrangement between the parties. The ability to have this opportunity will benefit their children by promoting the consistency and continuity of living in the family residence, keeping the same neighborhood friends, schools, and church.

6. The in-spouse will **maintain the property in the same condition** as when the Marital/Mediated Settlement Agreement is signed subject to normal wear and tear. The parties may consider hiring someone for the maintenance of the landscaping or pool. The out-spouse may be on a defined schedule to provide some maintenance service at the family residence that had been provided in the past, and is desired by the parties to continue until the home is divided. The parties may wish to factor the cost of these services in the support analysis, or as a reimbursement to be paid out of escrow on sale, or as part of the buy-out formula calculation. The parties may elect to reserve jurisdiction on the issues of maintenance and repairs.

7. The **maintenance and repair expenses** can be shared by mutual agreement to be defined between the parties. For example, the in-spouse will take care

of all repairs and maintenance items that cost less than $200, and the parties shall share equally the cost of repairs and maintenance above $200 by mutual agreement. If one spouse is financially unable to contribute to the repair and maintenance costs as required, then the other spouse shall pay and be reimbursed out of the escrow sales proceeds, or as otherwise decided by the parties, or as a factor in the buy-out formula, so that the residence can be maintained and repaired when required.

8. The parties shall be able to **sell their family residence** at any time by mutual agreement. This provides the parties with the greatest latitude to deal with unforeseen circumstances so that their interest in the property is protected.

9. **Define what will happen in the case of a party's death?** This may trigger a right of first refusal for the surviving party to purchase the decedent's interest from the estate of the decedent. If finances are slim and it would serve the children's best interest, then impose upon the estate of the decedent the specified term defined by the parties in their agreement for the sale of the home to maintain the continuity and consistency in the daily lives of the children. If the out- spouse is the survivor, the Mediated Settlement Agreement should shift the exclusive right of possession of the home to the out-spouse, as well as, the obligation to keep the payments in connection with the family residence current until divided between the survivor and the estate of the decedent, or until a buy-out of the estate's community interest in the family residence by the survivor parent, as provided for in the Agreement.

10. **When the in-spouse remarries or cohabits** this usually triggers a sale, or right of first refusal to buy-out the other party's community interest in the home. If there is a buy-out option, you can define that the parties will obtain a joint appraiser to obtain a fair market value, and then the parties can define the allowable deductions from the fair market value to complete the formula. The "buy-out" formula should be defined by the parties in their Agreement. Or, the parties may consider a modification of the support payments or shared expenses.

11. **Capital improvements to the family residence** may be required during the tenancy in common ownership, and how these costs shall be shared can be defined by mutual agreement. When one party is financially not able to contribute and the capital improvement is necessary or approved by mutual agreement, then the other spouse can pay for the improvement and be reimbursed out of the escrow sales proceeds, or as a factor in the buy-out formula, or by any other mutually defined method.

12. What if a **spouse loses their employment** during the Tenancy in Common? This event may trigger an immediate listing and sale of the family residence, or trigger the right of first refusal to buy-out the other party's interest in the home, and/or create a new reimbursement claim should one party make payments for the other obligated party related to the family residence, such as, the mortgage principal, mortgage interest, other encumbrances, taxes, insurance, maintenance, or repairs. Further, the parties may wish to create a security device for their

Agreement that replaces this loss of income to get the house payment made in a timely manner should the obligated party lose his or her job.

13. A **right of first refusal** can be arranged by the parties to coordinate the buy-out of the other party's interest in the family residence when a certain mutually defined event occurs (remarriage, loss of employment, ability to qualify for a loan, the term of the deferred ownership expires). If the party with right of first refusal does not elect to buy, then the parties may provide a second right to buy-out the first party, if the first party does not elect or does not qualify to buy-out the other party's interest, then the second party will be provided a short period of time to exercise his or her right to purchase the residence before it is listed for sale. This buy-out approach avoids the loss of funds paid for costs of a listed sale and potential capital gains tax. It may provide a unique and rare opportunity for one spouse to be a homeowner.

14. Is there **natural disaster protection?** If the home has substantial equity, then the parties should consider insurance, or become aware of the availability and cost of earthquake coverage to protect the community equity in the home. The cost for this protection should be considered as part of the overall support scheme, and as a potential expense to be shared by the parties, or as a payment to be reimbursed on sale or buy-out.

15. What if the party with exclusive possession of the residence **vacates the premises?** If the in-spouse chooses to vacate the family residence, the Agreement should provide that this act is defined as a substantial change in circumstances. One of

the options includes allowing the out-spouse the ability to take-over exclusive possession, which would affect the current payment of support and obligations in connection with the family residence. This may require a mutual meeting with a C.P.A. to adjust payments and support and to maximize income tax credits. The parties may agree that when the in-spouse vacates the family residence, that an advance written notice would be required to be made to the out- spouse, and that this may trigger a listed sale or buy-out of the in- spouse's community interest in the family residence by elected option.

16. When the in-spouse **rents a portion of the family** residence, the parties may decide how to treat that rent income by mutual agreement. The parties may wish to preclude the ability to rent a portion of the home, unless by mutual agreement as to the identity of the renter, amount of rent, and how to divide the rent income, and disclose the rent income for annual income tax filing.

   The collapse of the real estate market and the economy is forcing divorcing couples to consider a deferred sale of their family residence. A review of the considerations provided in this article may alleviate the unnecessary loss of the family residence and promote a successful division of this community asset.

CHAPTER 11

EMPLOYEE BENEFITS

What are Employee Benefits?

Whatever a party acquires by virtue of their employment, such as, accrued vacation time, sick leave, contributions to tax deferred savings plans, stock purchase plans and stock option grants, restricted stock units, medical, dental, vision and life insurance plans.

As for retirement plans, the tax deferred plans can be divided by special qualified orders. For example, tax deferred plans, defined contribution plans, like I.R.A., 401k, or 403b plans, can be divided by agreement between the parties so that an amount or percentage of the plan can be divided between the parties by a payment from the plan to the non-participant spouse, who will have the opportunity to roll-over the funds income tax free to an I.R.A. plan, or simply take the funds as income and declare the income in the year of receipt without penalty.

I.R.A. plans can be divided by a simple directive to the I.R.A.

Administrator. Language in the Marital Settlement Agreement identifying the I.R.A. and the requested distribution can be supportive of this approach, and allow for a distribution from this account to the non-employed spouse.

These tax-deferred savings accounts can be very helpful in paying community debt, or providing a source of funds for a down payment on a house when there are no other assets. It is always wise for the parties to review the ultimate income tax liability for this approach.

The parties can be creative with the funds, which must be assigned to the non-participant spouse. The parties can define how these funds are to be used, for example, to pay down the community debt or create a fund for a down payment on a new property, or to establish a financial cushion for making the transition from being married to maintaining a separate household.

Otherwise, the funds can be used to continue a source of retirement funds for each party, or one party, depending on the mutually agreed approach for the division of assets and debts between the parties.

Defined benefit retirement plans, usually require that the employed spouse reach a certain age before monthly payments can be made by the plan administrator to the retiree.

These plans are most often found in the government sector or with educational institutions, such as, military retirement plans, civil service retirement plans, city, county, or state plans, police, fire,

California State Teachers Retirement System (CalSTRS), and Public Employee Retirement System (PERS).

Many other private corporations are using stock plans, profit share plans, and 401k plans in place of the historical defined benefit pension plan due to the administrative costs associated with the defined benefit pension plans.

The statement balance is only one factor in identifying the community property value of a defined benefit pension plan.

Do not be misled by the account statement balance provided on an annual or semi-annual basis for the valuation of a defined benefit pension plan, this does not represent the community property value of the plan.

An actuary is needed to establish the community property value of these defined benefit pension plans.

This type of plan can be divided by finding the community property value of this asset with the assistance of an actuary, and then deciding whether to trade-off this asset with other assets, or provide a buy-out of the non-participant's share by the employee, or divide it under a time-rule formula (date of marriage to date of separation is the numerator and the date of hire to date of retirement as the denominator, the result is divided by 2, times (x) the gross monthly benefit). A court order, Qualified Domestic Relations Order (QDRO) is drafted and file to reflect the division of the monthly retirement benefit, so that each party will receive payments on a monthly basis when the employee qualifies for pension payments.

The in-kind division may actually occur many years in the future after the marital status has terminated. It is critical in many situations for the parties to join the retirement plan administrator, as a party to the divorce proceeding, especially before the marital status is terminated. By joining the retirement plan administrator, the plan is put on notice of the non-participant's interest in the retirement benefits, as well as, making the Plan administrator a party to the divorce proceeding so that the order defining the division of the retirement plan can be implemented by the Plan administrator and, if need be, enforced in court.

And, for Federal Civil Service and Military retirement plans, it is crucial to divide this plan by a Domestic Relations Order <u>before</u> the status of marriage is terminated to avoid losing the ability to divide this property in the state court where the divorce action is pending , when the pension is controlled by Federal law and not State law.

A consideration for the parties when a retirement plan is to be divided many years in the future is the fact that the spouse with the plan will have to wait to enjoy the benefits on a monthly basis, while in a buy-out, trade, or off-set, the non-participant spouse is enjoying the value immediately, and this should be a factor to consider when dividing this asset in any other manner, except the in-kind division, using the time-rule formula.

This parties should weigh one party's desire to have a complete and separate division of assets and debts. The economic situation of the parties, and any other unique considerations that can be shared by the parties.

Dividing Stock Options

Stock options represent employee compensation, generally used by a corporation to attract and keep qualified employees, and to share the profit of a corporation with its employee.

Determining when a stock options is earned is a fact specific determination, requiring a look at the reason why the corporation granted the options to the employee as well as the type of stock options granted. There is much confusion in the law about how to treat stock options granted for pure salary or bonus; deferred compensation in the form of pensions; deferred compensation in the form of contributions to a defined contribution plan; and, deferred income received through stock options.

Today, most courts consider stock options as a form of deferred compensation, and the non-participant spouse would have an interest in stock options granted during the marriage but vesting after the date of separation.

The parties in mediation should consider that the stock options not divisible as community property are available for support.

Stock options that are granted during the marriage and vest after the date of separation can be apportioned between the community property of the parties and the separate property of the employed spouse.

For example, Wife receives a grant of 4,000 shares on June 1, 2005 at a strike price of $5 per share, and which has a four-year vesting period. The grant provides that on June 1, 2006 = 1,000 shares will vest, and thereafter the 1,000 shares per year will vest annually (most plans will vest on a daily or monthly basis after one year) A "time rule" formula can be used to identify the community and separate property shares. The parties separate permanently on September 1, 2007.

Date of Grant to Date of Separation

> X # of shares vested = CP (community) shares

Date of Grant to Date of Vesting

1st year)6/1/2005 to 9/1/2007 = 27 mos.(date of grant to date of sep
    6/1/2005 to 6/1/2006 = 12 mos.(date of grant to date of ves
= 100% x 1,000 = 1,000 Community Property shares

2nd year) 27 mos.
    6/1/2005 to 6/1/2007= 24 mos
= 100% x 1,000 = 1,000 Community Property shares

3rd year) 27 mos.
    6/1/2005 to 6/1/2008 = 36 mos.
= 75% x 1,000 = 750 CP shares and 25 Separate Property Shares

4th year) 27 mos.
    6/1/2005 to 6/1/2009 = 48 mos.
= 56% x 1,000 = 560 CP shares and 440 SP shares

In this model for the division of the stock options between the parties, in the 3rd and 4th years of the Grant, the non employed spouse will have a pro rata share of the vesting stock. Under the example, if the stock has a value greater than $5, then as the shares vest, the non employed spouse will have the election to exercise and sell the stock options which have vested.

CHAPTER 12
PERSONAL PROPERTY

Dividing Personal Property

Some of the items in this category include automobiles, furniture, furnishings, appliances, jewelry, and art objects.

These items should be valued at fair market, and when the purchase is associated with a loan, secured by the item, then deduct the balance due on the loan for the net fair market value of the item when comparing the total value of personal property assigned to each party by their agreement.

These items can be appraised independently when extensive and valuable, or when there is confusion between the parties as to value. The Blue Book on the internet is available for vehicles. The division of personal property is usually accomplished by agreement between the parties, or by choosing items in an alternating fashion when there is a break down in agreement.

Vehicles (Kelly Blue Book website is a good source for value) and if the vehicle is secured by a loan then reduce the fair market value of the vehicle by the loan amount to the determine the net value (the parties can assign the vehicle and the loan payments to one party with an indemnity clause in the Mediation Agreement for the protection of the other party in the divorce proceeding). The vehicle is secured by a loan naming both parties, and the lender is not bound by the Mediation

Agreement indemnity, however, the other party is bound.

Tips For Dividing Personal Property

From the book <u>Your Divorce Advisor</u>, Diana Mercer, JD and Marsha Kline Pruett, PhD., MSL, provide a very good guide for parties entitled, "10 Tips on Personal Property":

1) Divide your personal property without the help of your lawyer or the court. Unless domestic violence is involved, it's not cost-effective to use lawyers or the court's time to divide your furniture and personal belongings. By the time you've fought about it, you could have purchased all new things!

2) Make an inventory of your household items, and decide what you would like from the list.

3) Speak with your spouse (provided domestic violence is not involved) about what he or she would like from the inventory. Are there items, which you can agree upon? If so, that part is settled.

4) Try and divide things based on what you both actually need. Courts rarely award money in lieu of a share of personal property, so unless you and your spouse agree on a buy-out for a specific item (or even the whole house full of furniture), you will receive personal property, not cash.

5) If you cannot agree on how to divide your list of items, try flipping a coin. One person picks first, the other second, and so on.

6) Try and divide the items sensibly. If your spouse has the children 75% of the time, maybe she/he should get the Wii game. If you need a computer for your business, that may take precedence over your child's desire to use the internet.

7) Gift items from family members ordinarily go back to the spouse to whom they were given. Grandma's hope chest goes to her grandchild, not her ex-grandchild-in-law.

8) Gift items between the two of you go to the original recipient. You don't get back the diamond Valentine pendant from 1995 just because you are splitting up now.

9) If pets are involved, try and make your judgment based on where the pet is better off. Does your spouse have a shorter workday, while you work 14 hours straight? Fido probably needs walks more often than you can realistically provide.

10) If it won't matter in 5 years, let it go. Are you too focused on a few specific items that won't change your life? Maybe each item is a symbol for something else . . . and it's time to let go.

CHAPTER 13

CHILD CUSTODY AND PARENTING

How Do We Tell the Children about the Divorce?

It is critical for divorcing parents to show a united front with their children to avoid the temptation to blame the other parent, and seek the alignment of the children with one parent against the other parent.

In the best interest of the children, it would be wise for the parents to tell their children in a family meeting about the divorce, and that

Father and Mother have a plan to share the children, love the children and support the children as their primary focus. Avoiding this process can generate feelings of confusion, betrayal and deception in the children.

Donald T. Saponsnek (www.mediate.com/dsaponsnek), in his article, "What Should We Tell the Children? Developing a Mutual

Story of the Divorce," suggests that the parents should develop a mutual story of the divorce, and to tell this story together to their children at the same time. This avoids each parent telling the children a totally different version of the divorce, and curtails a situation where the children believe that one parent is not telling the truth, or that one parent is to blame.

In this article, Mr. Saponsnek cites examples of marital situations and proposed mutual stories as an educational tool. Mr. Saponsnek recommends the following:

1. Tell your children the truth about the separation and divorce in advance;

2. Both parents should tell the children at the family home at a time that is distraction free, familiar and comfortable;

3. Use words that are addressed to the specific developmental level of your child. Talk to the children in simple words and phrases, and talk to adolescents in more adult ways;

4. Set aside enough time to answer questions about what is going to happen and how the children will be a priority for each parent in the future.

PLEASE SEE THE APPENDIX FOR BOOKS, WEBSITES AND AUDIO PROGRAMS FOR ADULTS AND CHILDREN

Determining Child Custody

Joint Custody means joint legal and joint physical custody. It is recommended that there be joint legal custody when parents are cooperative or wish to work toward being cooperative. Only in extreme conflict cases would there be a deviation from this concept, and this will fulfill the overall philosophy that children should have frequent and continuing contact with their parents. If both parents are healthy and capable of parenting their children, then it is presumed by law to be in the best interest of the children that the parents shall have joint legal and joint physical custody. There is no preference to a parent because of gender.

Joint Legal Custody means that both parents shall have the right and responsibility to make decisions relating to the health, education and welfare of the child. It means that both parents are legally responsible for the behavior of their children with or without limitation.

Joint Physical Custody means each parent shall have significant periods of physical custody. Physical custody is divided on an approximately equal basis. A typical 50/50 division would be to alternate one week with each parent, or a split where one parent gets Monday and Tuesday and the other parent gets Wednesday and Thursday and the parents alternate the weekends. Anything should be possible taking into consideration the children's school schedule, children's activities, and parent's work schedules. It is important to recognize that tender-aged children need more frequent contact, and it might not be in the best interest of a two-year old child to be on a week on/ week off schedule with the parents. Custody shall be shared in such a way so as to assure a child "frequent contact" with both parents. It would be imperative for the parents wishing to share joint physical custody to live near each other so that they can participate actively and efficiently with the children. Each parent would be able to take the children to school and pick up the children in a reasonable way. Children tend to remain loyal to both parents, and even though one parent is having difficulty accepting the other parent's role, joint parenting can work if the parents are flexible and remain attentive to the children.

<u>Sole Legal Custody</u> means that one parent shall make decisions relating to health, education, and welfare of the children. And, only in extreme conflict cases, or where one parent is not healthy (drug or alcohol abuser), should the parents resort to sole legal custody.

<u>Sole Physical Custody</u> means that the child shall reside under the supervision of one parent subject to the children visiting the other parent. The parents can establish a visitation plan that is generally between 15% and 30% timeshare with the children. A typical plan would provide for every other weekend with a mid week overnight, which is approximately 22% with the non-custodial parent. The parents can be as creative as their circumstances allow in establishing the parenting (visitation) plan

You will need to think about a parenting plan that meets the needs of your children and each parent.

To develop a plan, each parent will need to consider the school calendar, child activities, each parent's work schedule, vacations, work holidays, and school holidays.

Depending on the age of the children, each parent's proximity to the children's school, and the existence of healthy cooperation and communication between the parents, an extremely simple agreement can be created to share children. Otherwise, the parties can define their parenting plan to include a division of major holidays.

Parents may use a website calendar to define their timeshare and child/school activities, parties, field trips, practice schedules, medical and dental appointments, and as a safeguard and constant reminder of the parenting plan.

Each parent, and age appropriate children, can add information to the website calendar for the benefit of each parent and the children.

There are websites for exploring Parenting Plans:

1. www.extension.umn.edu/parentsforever

2. http://www.alaska.net/~akctlib/forms.htm (parenting plans)

3. www.nolo.com (parenting agreement)

4. ShareKids.com (Website to set-up a calendar defining the parenting plan, special events, doctor & dentist appointments)

5. http://www.divorce-education.com

6. http://www.OurFamilyWizard.com This is a website calendar displaying the parenting plan schedule, doctor and dental appointments, practice and game schedules, prescription medicine and procedures, and any other information relevant for the parents and children to know and share with each other.

7. LifeMatters.com (Tools for Stress less Parenting)

8. www.divorceinfo.net/coparent.html (Sample of Co-parenting agreement).

9. www.ncoft.gse.upenn.edu The Co-parenting library.

10. www.yahoo.com (Shared Calendar)

Parenting and Time Share Agreements

You will need to think about a parenting plan that meets the needs of your children and the parents. You will need the following information to begin the process:

1. A yearly calendar showing holidays
2. A school calendar showing school events and holidays

The parent's work schedules, which include each parent's vacations and holidays.

Simple Parenting Agreements: These work well when the parents are cooperative and each parent promotes sharing the children with flexibility. Mother/Father has primary physical custody subject to the other parent having reasonable physical custody. Or, the parents to have joint physical custody with the children which promotes a substantially equal timeshare as agreed between the parents. If the children are older, then the parents may wish to establish physical care and custody as agreed upon between the child(ren) and Father/Mother with advance notice to the other parent.

Structured Parenting Agreements: These Agreements involve detailed terms, which establish the limits of each parent's rights and responsibilities.

1) General Parenting Plan:
   a) Weekends (alternate every other weekend, or 1st, 3rd & 5th and 2nd and 4th.
   b) Selected times during the school week and either the same schedule or a different schedule for the summer recess. The parents will define

the overnight schedule, looking for a more frequent exchange for children of tender years.

2. Specific Holidays and Summer Vacation

   a) Thanksgiving day and Thanksgiving weekend

   b) Christmas eve, Christmas day, and Christmas recess

   c) Easter

   d) Spring break

   e) 4th of July

   f) Mother's and Father's day

   g) Mother's and Father's birthday

   h) Child(ren)'s birthday(s)

   i) 3-day weekends: President's day, Memorial day, Labor day, Martin Luther King day

   j) Summer vacation

Christmas Holiday example: The first day of Christmas recess until 12/25 at 2pm to Mother in odd years and Father in even years. From 12/25 at 2pm until return to school to Father in odd years and Mother in even years.

Summer vacation example: Each parent to have two consecutive weeks in the summer for a vacation with the children. Each parent will notify the other parent in writing, by May 15 of each year, of their two weeks vacation schedule. If there is a conflict, then Mother prevails in odd years and Father prevails in even years.

Other topics to consider:

1) Pick up and drop off times and location (authorized parties to provide this service)

2) Transportation responsibility: Will it be shared? Each parent driving one way; or alternate; will the parents meet ½ way between their homes (at a McDonalds, bookstore, park); or at day care or school to exchange the children.

3) Each parent to keep the other informed of their employment and work schedule, and report any changes within 72 hours.

4) Other cultural or celebrated holidays.

5) If not joint, then designate decision making authority for the children's education, medical & dental care.

6) Each parent to keep the other informed of their current address and phone number.

7) Telephone access for the children and parents.

8) Conditions for taking the children out of the state may include prior notice, itinerary, addresses and phone numbers.

9) Prohibition for the parents to refrain from speaking in a derogatory manner about the other parent in the presence of the children.

10) Terms for religious training and/or education

11) Right of first refusal, in preference to a child care provider, when the custodial parent is unavailable for an extended period of time

12) If the children are sick and unable to attend school. Who will be responsible for the care of the children?

13) Is the schedule appropriate for the age of the children?

Parenting After the Divorce

Florence Bienenfield, Ph.D., in her article, "Helping Your Child Succeed After Divorce," provides the following information for parents:

1. See your child as soon as possible after the physical separation from your spouse.

2. Encourage your child to have a positive relationship with the other parent.

3. See your child regularly.

4. Gain your child's trust.

5. Do not try to turn your child against the other parent.

6. Don't pressure your child to choose where he or she wants to live.

7. Avoid discussion with your child of legal and financial matters pertaining to the divorce.

8. Cooperate when there is an emergency or crisis.

9. Seek therapeutic help for your child if certain symptoms persist (depression or poor grades or withdrawal).

<u>Creating a Closer Relationship with Your Child</u>

1. Become a good listener

2. Allow your child to fully express feelings

3. Comfort and Reassure your child

4. Go ahead and show your affection for your child

5. Protect your child from parental disputes or disagreements

6. Set reasonable rules and limits for your child's behavior according to her or his age and development

7. Along with discipline, give your children as much praise as you can

8. Do not call your child names or use put-downs.

9. Set realistic goals for your child

10. Avoid excessive behavior

11. Spend some leisure time and play with your child

12. Gradually, patiently, and with love, help your child learn and grow.

Guidelines For Parents To Help Diminish Conflict

Santa Clara County (California) Family Court Services has provided the following guidelines for divorcing parents:

Do not discuss any issues with the other parent in the presence of the children; limit your conversation when the children are exchanged to a simple "hello" and "goodbye."

Any phone calls about the children should be limited to only that topic; tell the other parent in advance whether you are calling to discuss the children or some other issue.

Do not send messages for the other parent through your child; talk to the other parent directly, by phone, by email, or mail.

Be very clear with each other about your plans for time with the children, include specific dates and times. Do not change any plans without first calling or discussing the proposed change with the other parent in advance.

To be sure each parent has the same information, follow up the discussion of an arrangement or agreement in writing and send a copy to the other parent.

Talk to teachers, doctors, or other involved professionals to help resolve differences of opinion about what is best for your children.

Each parent is responsible for their children's daily care when they are with them. Parents must consult with each other regarding changes in the child's educational and medical care, in advance of the change.

Co-Parenting Tips

"Mediation becomes a Key Way to Heal Children of Divorce," an article written by Melinda Sacks, Mercury News Staff Writer, and provides that therapists offer these suggestions to divorcing parents:

1. Don't be afraid to let your child love the other parent. Worries about "losing the child" are unfounded, say the therapists. The worst thing to do is force a child to choose one parent over the other.

2. Don't fight in front of the children—no matter what.

3. Don't "put down" the other parent.

4. Don't assume because you don't like your ex-spouse, your child won't like or love him or her.

5. Don't tell your children something about why you are getting divorced. Even the youngest child can be given a simple explanation:

   "Mommy and Daddy don't get along." There is no need to go into great detail, but children worry it is their fault if they are told nothing.

   (See "How Do We Tell the Children About the Divorce," above p. 105)

6. Give children liberal access to both parents.

7. Let kids talk about the divorce and their feelings without the parent getting upset.

8. Recognize there is grief, especially at times of transition.

9. Tell the children you will not be getting back together with your ex-spouse if this is the case. Many children believe if they are just good enough, their parents will reunite.

10. Find a support or discussion group for your child (many are being offered through public schools) to address the feeling of aloneness many feel.

Michelle H. Cauley, JaNan Davis, and Marcia Barnes, created a handbook entitled "From Parent Wars to Co-Parenting," and in their handbook there are:

<u>Ten Tips for Co-Parenting</u>

1. Make your child's happiness and well being your number one joint goal.

2. Treat the other parent in a business like manner.

3. Treat your child as a child, not as an adult, confidant, messenger, or spy.

4. Encourage your child as a child's relationship with the other parent.

5. Communicate directly with the other parent.

6. Make visitation exchanges pleasant and happy.

7. Take a co-parenting class.

8. Pay your child support on time.

9. Be patient and flexible.

10. Get family counseling, if you need it.

These tips are from "From Parent Wars to Co-Parenting," by Michelle H. Cauley, JaNan Davis, and Marcia Barnes.

More Considerations for Co-Parenting

An article written by Donna Leigh Yanish provides the following advice for parents:

1. Always put your children's interests first.

2. Show your children that the parents respect each other.

   "Dissing your ex serves no useful purpose."

3. Encourage the kids' relationship with their other parent.

4. Avoid the temptation to be nosy—whom your ex is dating is none of your business.

5. Don't use the children as messengers, especially for support checks. Protect your kids from those exchanges.

6. As much as possible, reduce conflict and pick up the children at a neutral spot such as school or day care.

7. If the children are very young when a parent moves out, make sure they see where he or she is living. They need to see that the parent is safe.

8. Don't ask your children to split their loyalties. If you start a sentence with "Don't tell your dad (or mom) this . . . . .," you're headed for trouble.

9. Discuss rules for the kids so that, as much as feasible, you can present a united front. This is especially important with teenagers. The more they see their parents disagreeing, the more opportunities they have to take advantage of the situation. Said one therapist: "Children of divorced parents develop enormous manipulation skills that can be disastrous if they get into trouble with drugs and sex. For parents, that can be a great motivator to get along."

An important tool for parents separated by a great distance, which means that contact is not as frequent, is to use a web-cam (Skype) to be able to view the children when you speak with them. Purchase a mutual subscription to a magazine of mutual interest to share information.

CHAPTER 14

SUPPORT

Calculating a Child Support Amount

It is the general obligation of both parents to support their minor children in the manner suitable to the child's circumstances. There is a statewide uniform Child Support Guideline based upon the principles that a parent's first obligation is to support his or her minor children according to the parent's circumstances and station in life.

Both parents are mutually responsible for the support of their children.

California courts are required by federal law to impose a uniform guideline approach in calculating child support. Child Support payments specified in the Agreement or divorce decree or separation instrument are not included in the recipient's gross income or deducted from the payor's income for income tax reporting. The money is for the benefit and welfare of the children.

Parents in a mediation setting will analyze and define the amount of child support, which will fit their circumstances.

However, in their Settlement Agreement it will be noted that the parties were informed and understand the Uniform Guideline amount for child support. When there is a change from the Uniform Guideline amount, then the court in California requires an attached calculation of the Uniform Guideline amount ("Dissomaster" and "Xspouse" are two examples of software programs used to determine the monthly Uniform Guideline amount of child support).

There are general standards to review when applying the uniform guideline for child support as follows:

1. A parent's principal and first obligation is to support his or her minor children according the parent's circumstances and station in life.

2. Both parents are mutually responsible for the support of their children.

3. Each parent's actual income and level of responsibility for the children is considered.

4. Each parent should pay for the support of their children according to his or her ability.

5. The interests of the child take top priority.

6. Children should share in the standard of living of both parents. Child support may improve the standard of living of the custodial household to improve the lives of the children.

7. Child support in cases in which both parents have high levels of responsibility for the children should reflect the increased costs of raising the children in two homes and should minimize significant disparities in the children's living standards in the two homes.

8. The financial needs of the children should be met through private resources as much as possible.

9. It is presumed that a parent having primary physical responsibility for the children contributes a significant portion of available resources for the support of the children.

10. The guideline is intended to be presumptively correct in all cases, and only under special circumstances should child support orders fall below the child support mandated by the guideline formula.

11. The child support amount must insure that children actually receive fair, timely, and sufficient support reflecting California's high standard of living and high costs of raising children compared to other states.

Calculating a Spousal Support Amount

As a general rule, for so long as husband and wife are living together, they owe each other a mutual duty of support.

The philosophy of the state of California for a permanent spousal support award is that the supported party should be allowed a period of time to make a transition from being married to living as a single person and becoming self-supporting. The court is required to consider all of the following circumstances below when making an order of spousal support in a contested case. The court is supporting a goal that the supported party shall be self-supporting within a reasonable period of time. A reasonable period of time for purposes of this section generally shall be one-half the length of the marriage.

However, nothing in this section is intended to limit the court's discretion to order support for a greater or lesser length of time, based on any of the other factors listed in this section and the circumstances of the parties.

A general determination for a spousal support award will take into consideration the parties' circumstances in reference to the standard of living established during their marriage and their respective needs and ability to pay.

"Standard of Living" can be determined by evaluating the earnings of each party during the last several years of the marriage ("income approach"), as well as, reviewing a history of the expenses of the parties ("the expense approach").

There is a presumption that the earning capacity of each party is sufficient to meet the standard of living during the marriage when considering the following factors:

1. The marketable skills of the supported party, and whether education or training is necessary or the development of new skills with education or training are required to assist the supported party to become self-supporting.

2. Has the supported party's earning capacity been impaired by periods of unemployment during the marriage to permit time for domestic duties?

3. The extent to which the supported party contributed to the attainment of an education, training, a career, or license for the supporting party.

4. The ability of the supporting party to pay support when assessing earning capacity, earned and unearned income, assets, and standard of living.

5. The needs of each party compared to the marital standard of living.

6. The obligations and assets of each party, including separate property.

7. The duration of the marriage.

8. The ability of the supported party to engage in gainful employment.

9. Age and health of the parties, and to what extent does the health of a party affect their earning capacity.

10. Is there a documented history of domestic violence?

11. Are there any immediate and specific tax consequences to each party.

12. How are the hardships balanced between the parties?

13. The supported spouse shall become self supporting in a reasonable time, generally ½ the term of the marriage **for s**horter marriages, and in long-term marriages (10 years or more), it is another factor for the parties to consider.

14. Any other factors which are just and reasonable may be considered by the parties in determining the need and/or amount of support.

With respect to divorce or separation Agreements executed by the parties, any payment between spouses or former spouses will qualify as alimony (taxable to recipient and deductible to payor) if all of the following tests are met:

1. Payment is made in cash (money order & checks payable on demand).

2. Payments must be received by or on behalf of the payee spouse (e.g., rent, mortgage, tax, or tuition liabilities of the payee spouse).

3. The payments are made under a divorce or separation instrument.

4. The payments are not designated as not includable in the income of the payee spouse and deductible by the payor spouse.

5. Spouses who are divorced or legally separated must not be members of the same household when the payment is made.

6. Liability to pay terminates on the death of the payee spouse.

7. The payor spouse and payee spouse must not file a joint income tax return together for the year in which payment occurred.

8. Payments must not be considered child support.

Spousal support payments made to the recipient shall be included as income in the year of receipt, and deducted from the income of the payor, for income tax reporting.

Calculating a Family Support Amount

An Agreement that is silent as to a child support amount, and spousal support amount is valid and shall create a form of support identified as "family support." The child support and spousal support are reserved with no designation as to amount.

Now, if properly worded, family support can be totally deductible as alimony by the payor, and must be reported as income by the payee on their income tax returns.

This approach to support can be very helpful when parties wish to retain a family residence as tenants in common, and the spouse living in the family residence can pay the mortgage principle and interest and taxes and take the allowable deductions on his or her income tax return, while the payor (the "out-spouse" – not living in the family residence) can deduct 100% of the support payments made to the party living in the family residence as an alimony expense on his or her income tax return.

The parties are able to maximize their income and income tax deductions in this situation, or, it should be avoided, as the IRS may wish to scrutinize the terms of the Agreement so that the family support can be defined as child support in order to defeat the alimony deduction.

The party paying the mortgage interest and real estate tax can deduct those payments on their income tax return and the party paying the family support deducts those payments on their income tax return as alimony. This is a win-win for the parties. They may be able to retain and defer the division of their family residence this way to allow their children to complete their education in the same school and to avoid the total disruption of the children's lives due to the divorce.

The legal requirements to qualify a family support payment from one spouse to another spouse as an alimony payment are as follows:

1) The payment is received by or on behalf of a spouse under a marital settlement agreement, temporary order, or other written agreement.

2) The instrument does not designate the payment as not being includable in the recipient's gross income and not deductible by the payor.

3) The spouses are not members of the same household when the family support payment is made.

4) No liability exists to make the payment-or any substitute payment for any period after the spouse's death.

Registered Domestic Partners

The same terms and conditions of the California Family Code apply equally to same sex partners registered as domestic partners and opposite sex partners. At this time, Domestic Partners face difficulties when confronted with federal law and procedure.

Basic areas of concern include:

1. Filing Income Tax returns: For tax years beginning after 12/31/2006, a California registered domestic partner must report 1/2 of the community income, whether received in the form of compensation for personal services or income from property, on his or her federal income tax return. For tax years beginning before

6/1/2010, registered domestic partners may, but are not required to, amend their returns to report income in accordance with the Chief Counsel Advisory, 201021050 (5/28/2010).

2. Real Estate Ownership: When registered or legally married same sex couples acquire community property real estate, and one partner dies, then the other party will not have the step-up in basis of the property otherwise available to opposite sex married couples.

3. Estate Planning: There is no unlimited marital deduction, so the deceased same sex partner's estate is immediately subject to Federal Estate Tax, which could otherwise be deferred as it is for opposite sex married couples.

4. Social Security: For parties married for more than 10 years, enhanced social security benefits are available to qualified opposite sex couples, but not to same sex partners.

5. At this time only a few states recognize same sex marriage, as such, it may preclude same sex couples from living in any other states that do not recognize the marriage.

6. Important Resource Materials for Registered Domestic Partnerships include:

    a) FTB Publication 737: Tax Information for Registered Domestic Partners.

    b) FTB Q&A: What if I'm a domestic partner?

    c) FTB Publication 2429: Alimony Frequently Asked Questions.

CHAPTER 15
A DIVORCE MEDIATION MODEL

The mediation process is unique to the parties and their circumstances. The process is defined and driven by the parties and their chosen and defined topics. The following outline of the mediation process is not controlling and serves as a model and platform for the parties to explore.

First Mediation Session (1 to 2 hours)

This begins with a comparative explanation about the mediation process, the collaborative process and litigation. This is followed by a question and answer session for the parties. Some mediators may require a conflict questionnaire to be filled-in, or other evaluative information from the parties to set the stage and ground rules for mediation. This session provides an opportunity to get to know each party and the mediator.

The parties and mediator enter into an agreement or acknowledgment and consent for mediation, which defines the duties of the mediator and the parties, the fee for mediation services, and the procedure for mediation.

Next, the parties will list and share their concerns, worries, visions, and goals for the mediation process without any judgment.

It is important that this initial process is free from judgment, comment, and reaction to insure that each party is heard. This will be the basis for starting the communication between the parties in a safe setting with reasonable boundaries. It is important that each party is able to communicate their goals, wishes and desires in the form of "I messages" instead of "you" or "we" messages.

Then, the parties will be encouraged to describe any immediate concerns or topics to be discussed and resolved together, such as, temporarily paying obligations and sharing the children. It may take a few weeks to finalize an agreement to divide property and debts, resolve support, custody, and establish a parenting plan.

The parties may need to find a way to insure how common bills are to be paid, property maintained, and parenting the children on a temporary basis, until the parties can adopt a more formal parenting plan.

The parties will be introduced to the Declaration of Disclosure requirement. These forms list and define all assets, debts, income and expenses. A <u>full and complete disclosure</u> is required from each party. In addition, the parties shall keep each other informed of any material changes to the Declaration of Disclosure information during the mediation process, such as, the receipt of a bonus, commission, or a raise in income after the date of separation. A general discussion of community and separate property, as well as, fair market value is important for the parties to understand before they begin to prepare these forms. The need for an appraiser to determine fair market value for certain assets, such as, real estate, pension plan, or a business will become more apparent. The parties may discuss different ways to value an asset, including the use of an independent appraiser.

Legal Procedure at the First Mediation Session:

1. Sign an acknowledgment and consent for mediation, or any other agreement provided by the mediator for the Mediation process. This is a contract defining the fees and costs, confidentiality of the process, and disclaimers regarding representation (the mediator may also be a family law attorney), limitations

of the mediator to hire independent investigators or initiate discovery of the nature, extent, value, and amount of community, quasi-community and separate property.

2. Review the current estate plan with the parties by identifying joint tenancy property, existing wills, or a revocable family trust for revocation and/or amendment, according to the wishes and desires of the participants. Check to avoid a "due on sale clause" in a secured loan if the title to the property is changed.

    The parties to be provided an opportunity to review and discuss any Amendments, or modifications at the next mediation session so that they each can make a new temporary estate plan.

    The parties may be referred to independent estate planning counsel to ensure estate plan wishes are drafted and accomplished during the mediation process and through the entry of Judgment and termination of the marital status, if required by the parties.

3. The introduction and explanation of the Declaration of Disclosure (schedule of Assets and Debts and Income and Expense

Declaration). This is a Prerequisite to discussing and finalizing the terms and conditions of the division of the property, and the resolution of support. California law requires that in every divorce proceeding, each side must complete a disclosure of all assets and debts of the marriage. You must disclose all property of any nature, including real property, tangible and intangible property, such as, stocks, stock options, bonds, or investment opportunities, job offers, business opportunities, whether existing or contingent.

The mediator will provide these forms to the parties to prepare in advance of the mediation Session 2 or Session 3. Some mediators will provide completed explanatory sample forms for the parties. A one page declaration under penalty of perjury that these documents were exchanged between the parties is required by law (California), and is a prerequisite to signing a Stipulated Judgment or Mediated

Settlement Agreement, or filing a Judgment for Dissolution of Marriage.

The mediator will memorialize the information discussed, goals, and any temporary agreements in an email to the parties.

<u>Second Mediation Session (1 to 2 hours)</u>

The attorney mediator to provide a quick review of the legal process and required legal paperwork. The parties will need to approve the preparation and filing of a family law Summons, Petition and if there are minor children then a pleading defining where the children have resided for the last five years and with whom.

The parties shall decide who will be the Petitioner (the party filing the request for the divorce with the court), and the Petitioner's name shall be placed on the pleadings filed with the court as "self- represented."

A review and clarification of each party's concerns, worries, and goals.

The parties shall identify and provide an agenda of topics for discussion. The topics to be ranked in priority for discussion by the parties.

The resolution of the agenda items, including a follow-up on each party's plan for their estate planning changes, if at all.

A review of the Declaration of Disclosure forms, and resolution of questions regarding character of assets and the potential need for an appraisal to define the value of an asset.

A review of the current parenting plan, and how each parent's goal for parenting is being met.

Legal Procedure for the Second Mediation Session:

1. The parties to decide on who will be the Petitioner.

    The Petitioner's name will appear on the pleadings filed with the court. Many couples ask, "Is there is any advantage to being named as the Petitioner?" With regard to mediation, there is no advantage.

    However, in a litigated case, the Petitioner would be allowed to introduce evidence on contested issues first.

    California is a no-fault divorce jurisdiction. The Petitioner and Respondent cannot be blamed or punished in any manner for requesting a dissolution of their marriage.

2. Preparation and filing of the Petition, Summons and if minor children of the marriage, then a Child Custody Jurisdiction form, which identifies the residences of the minor children for the last five years, and with whom the children resided.

    Some parties in a mediation setting will decide to use a private divorce center to prepare all of their pleadings for filing with the court, except the Agreement or a Stipulated Judgment which identifies the division of their property and debts, resolves permanent support and custody of the children.

Each party has been provided a Schedule of Assets and Debts as well as an Income and Expense declaration to take home and fill-in for mediation sessions #2 and #3, depending on the complexity of the assets and debts, and goals of the parties.

An email will be sent to both parties identifying the information raised in the session, legal procedures and documents discussed, and any temporary agreements made by the parties.

Third Mediation Session (1 to 2 hours)

Itemization of topics to be discussed by the parties, then define an agenda for the session.

Respondent may be served the filed initial pleadings by the mediator (Both parties are provided filed endorsed copies at the same time in the mediation session). There would be no need to hire a process server!

The "date of service" commences the six-months waiting period for the parties to terminate their marital status in California.

Termination of the marital status will trigger three major topics:

First, the medical, dental, and vision benefits made available by group insurance plans provided by an employed spouse will terminate, as the non-employed spouse is no longer a dependent due to the termination of the marital status on the filing a Judgment for Dissolution of Marriage.

Second, the former spouses will not be able to file joint income tax returns together in the year that their status of marriage is terminated.

Third, the parties may wish to create a 10 years marriage to qualify for derivative social security benefits.

Therefore, the parties need to consider options for medical and dental coverage. The federal law under C.O.B.R.A. provides one option for the other spouse to retain coverage as an individual with the group carrier for up to three (3) years, an extremely important option if the dependent spouse has a serious prior existing medical condition, which might make it difficult to qualify independently for medical insurance. It may be financially beneficial to extend the date of termination of the marriage beyond the minimal six-months period so that the parties can file joint income tax returns for one more year, or to allow for any major medical or dental procedures to be completed under the employed spouse's group insurance coverage.

Also, the parties may wish to create a 10 years marriage for social security derivative benefits (under federal law the date of marriage to the date of marital status termination defines the term of the marriage).

Legal Procedure for the Third Mediation Session:

1. The Mediator may serve Respondent and Petitioner with filed endorsed copies of the Petition, Summons, and U.C.C.J.E.A. (minor children) forms, if this was not accomplished in the Second Mediation session. The parties to review any automatic temporary restraining orders identified in the Summons.

2. Prepare and file Proof of Service of Summons, Petition and U.C.C.J.E.A. forms. The <u>date of service</u> on this proof of service will identify that Respondent was served on this date, and the six (6) months waiting period to terminate the marital status commences on this date and not the date of filing of the Summons and Petition.

3. Review, complete, and exchange the Preliminary Declarations of Disclosure. Prepare Declaration of Disclosure face sheets and Declarations regarding Proof of Service of Declaration of Disclosure and file with the court.

    An email will be sent to both parties identifying the information raised in the session, agreements entered into, and procedural concerns.

Fourth Mediation Session (1 to 2 hours)

Identify and prioritize topics for discussion. Review and discuss assets and debts division, income and expenses for each party, and the parenting plan.

Resolve property character issues (separate or community property), the value of property to be divided, and options for the division of property and debts.

The parties to identify reimbursement claims for discussion and resolution.

If time allows then introduce the topics of custody and a parenting plan to the participants.

Legal Procedures for the Fourth Mediation Session:

1. Start a rough draft of the property settlement agreement or stipulated judgment, including topics discussed and resolved, and reserving topics unresolved for further discussion.

A lawyer will be needed to draft the Marital or Mediated Settlement Agreement, or Stipulated Judgment. The parties may opt for their mediator (if a family law attorney) to draft the agreement, and the parties should then be provided adequate time to review the agreement terms and conditions with an independent family law attorney. Further, at any time in the mediation process the parties shall have the opportunity to review any topic with a family law lawyer to keep informed of their rights.

Further, an outline of the terms and conditions of the Agreement can be provided by the mediator to the parties, and a Marital Settlement Agreement can be drafted by a chosen family law attorney, and this document may be reviewed by each party's independent family law counsel.

An email memorializing the session is sent to both parties, reviewing the information discussed, agreements made, and procedural topics resolved.

Fifth Mediation Session (1 to 2 hours)

Set agenda items with participants. And, after the property division is resolved, reimbursement claims identified and resolved, custody defined and the parenting plan defined, then identify the required

Guideline used for child support and Guideline child support amount using the Income and Expense declarations prepared by the parties.

Review the financial expenses of each party, and identify Guideline child support. The parties will agree on the child support amount, emphasizing their income and expenses, needs, goals, and factors for making the transition from one household with combined incomes and expenses to separate households with individual income and expenses, using the Guideline as only one factor. Or, if the parties agree, they will use the Guideline as the child support amount.

Then, the parties should review the spousal support factors. The same Software program that the parties used to define Guideline child support will display a formula for identifying "temporary" spousal support. It would be an error of law for the court to solely use this computer calculation for a permanent spousal support award, but it may prove helpful as one of the factors to review when the parties decide on the amount of the permanent spousal support award.

These software programs ("Dissomaster" and "Xspouse") provide useful information about net adjusted income for the parties and net spendable income after taxes and support is paid.

In this process, the parties will review their expenses and income and relate this to their goals, and to support each other's transition from being married with combined incomes and expenses to being separate with individual income and expenses.

Legal Procedure for the Fifth Mediation Session:

1. The Mediator will update the proposed Agreement for division of property and obligations; the arrangement for custody and parenting plan; the child support amount; and, a discussion on permanent spousal support factors. The parties will be given the opportunity and time to review the updated proposed terms and conditions of their Agreement or Stipulated Judgment with independent family law counsel.

2. Prepare and Exchange Final Declarations of Disclosure, or use the Waiver of Final Declaration of Disclosure procedure.

An email will be sent memorializing the information discussed, procedural concerns, and any agreements made by the parties.

<u>Sixth Mediation Session (1 to 2 hours)</u>

Final review of proposed rough draft Agreement or Stipulated

Judgment, and finalize the settlement scenarios for property division, custody and parenting plan, child and spousal support. Make final agreement on all terms and conditions.

The parties to be allowed the opportunity to review the final

Marital Settlement Agreement or Stipulated Judgment with independent family law counsel.

<u>Legal Procedure for the Sixth Mediation Session:</u>

1. The parties to return and sign the final draft Marital Settlement Agreement or Stipulated Judgment after review with independent family law counsel, and prepare a Request to Enter Default (file only after the parties have signed the Marital Settlement Agreement . . . this approach allows the parties to save the filing fee for a Response) However, some Counties find that by signing the Marital Settlement Agreement and merging the Agreement into a Judgment for Dissolution of Marriage that this act is an appearance and the filing fee will be required. And, in that case, you will use an Appearance, Stipulation and Waiver form, instead of the Request to Enter Default form.

2. Either prepare Final Declarations of Disclosure or a Waiver of the Final Declarations of Disclosure.

3. Prepare a Declaration for Uncontested Judgment form (jurisdictional facts are confirmed by declaration under penalty of perjury, and there is no need for a personal appearance by the Petitioner at court).

4. Prepare a Judgment form, which is the Decree for Dissolution of Marriage and the Marital Settlement Agreement terms and conditions are attached to this form and merged into a Judgment for Dissolution of Marriage.

5. Prepare a Notice of Entry of Judgment form which recites the date of the entry for the Judgment for Dissolution of Marriage and the date of the termination of the marital status. This form is mailed directly to the parties from the court.

6. Some jurisdictions require a Child Support Case Registry form. When there are minor children, the County may require this form to be prepared and filed which provides statistical information about each parent.

    In many jurisdictions these documents can be filed as a packet with the Document Examiner in the Family Division of the Superior Court. The Petitioner will not have to make an appearance in court.

7. This may constitute the final session, and the parties will sign the Marital Settlement Agreement or Stipulated Judgment. They will review the final legal process for submitting the "judgment packet" to the document examiner. The Mediator will resolve final questions and concerns of the parties. Upon receipt of the filed endorsed judgment packet from the court, then the Mediator will remind the parties of the termination of the marital status date; the possible need for the unemployed or formerly covered spouse to request medical insurance

coverage under C.O.B.R.A. Allow for confirmation that all independent orders required to divide employee tax deferred accounts and defined benefit pension/retirement plans have been drafted and lodged with the Plan administrators. Finally, the Mediator will remind the parties to review their estate plans.

8. Draft a Proof of Service to verify delivery to each party of the filed endorsed Judgment for Dissolution of Marriage.

9. Draft a Final letter to parties verifying the marital status termination date; if pertinent, the order required for the division of employee benefits, if not already divided; party's health coverage plans, confirm or change the beneficiary designation for life insurance and other assets to be paid on death; a reminder of the agreed income tax filing status if the parties are deferring their marital status to file a joint income tax return; and, a reminder for an estate plan review.

10. An email shall be prepared and sent to both parties defining the activity of the parties at this session.

APPENDIX

Books for Parents

1. The Good Karma Divorce, Avoid Litigation, Turn Negative Emotions into Positive Actions, and Get on with the Rest of Your Life, Judge Michele Lowrance.

2. The Co-Parent Survival Guide, Elizabeth S. Thayer, Ph.D. and Jeffrey Zimmerman, Ph.D.

3. Making Divorce Easier on Your Child: 50 Effective Ways to Help Children Adjust, Nicholas Long, Ph.D. and Rex Forehand, Ph.D.

4. American Bar Association Handbooks:

    a) The Never-Ending Divorce

    b) Surviving Your Divorce

    c) Co-Parents After Divorce

    d) My Parents are Getting a Divorce ABA Publication Orders, PO Box 10892, Chicago, IL 6061—0892 (1800-285-2221

5. Parenting After Divorce, A Guide to Resolving Conflicts and Meeting Your Children's Needs, Philip M. Stahl, Ph.D.

6. Ex-Etiquette For Parents, Jan Blackstone

7. <u>Helping Children Cope with Divorce,</u> Edward Teyber

8. <u>Divorce Poison</u>, Richard A. Warshak

9. <u>Mom's House, Dad's House,</u> Isolina Ricci

10. <u>Step-Wives,</u> 10 Steps to help ex-wives and stepmothers end the struggle and put the kids first, Lynne Oxhorn-Ringwood and Marjorie Vego Krausz, ED.D., M.E.T.

11. <u>Child Custody-Building Arrangements that Work,</u> Mimi Lyster

12. <u>Creative Divorce,</u> Mel Krnatzler

13. <u>The Custody Solutions Sourcebook,</u> Jan Blackstone

14. <u>The Divorce Book,</u> Matthew McKay

15. <u>Divorce Help Sourcebook,</u> Margorie Engel

16. <u>For the Sake of the Children,</u> Kris Kline

17. <u>Getting Ready to Negotiate-</u>"The Getting to Yes TM Workbook," Rodger Fisher and Danny Ertel

18. <u>The Joint Custody Handbook,</u> Miriam Cohen

19. <u>Letting Go,</u> Dr. Zev Wanderer & Tracy Cabot

20. <u>Mediating Child Custody Disputes,</u> Donald Saponsnek

21. <u>Mediation,</u> Jay Folber & Alison Taylor

22. <u>Vicki Lansky's Divorce Book for Parents,</u> Vicki Lansky

23. <u>The Good Divorce,</u> Constance Ahrons, Ph.D.

24. <u>We're Still Family,</u> Constance Ahrons, Ph.D.

25. <u>Conscious Divorce, Ending a Marriage with Integrity,</u> Susan Allison

26. <u>Children Heard, I Love You More than Chocolate</u>, Marcia Tabram Philips

27. <u>The Best of Both Nests</u>, Jane Clark

28. <u>Blending Families</u>, Elaine Fantle Shimberg

29. <u>Families Apart: Ten Keys to Successful Co-Parenting</u>, M. Blau

30. <u>Single Father's Handbook</u>, Richard H. Gatley, Ph.D. & David Koulack, Ph.D.

31. <u>Women, Divorce and Money</u>, Mary Rogers

32. <u>After You've Said Good-Bye, Learning How to Stand Alone</u>, Trudy Helminger

33. <u>Co-Parenting—Joint Custdoy, A Source book for the Separated or Divorced Family</u>, Marion Golper

34. "40 Ways to Help Your Youngster Achieve in School," Better Homes and Gardens (March 1985), Dan Kaercher

35. <u>101 Ways to be a Long Distance Super Dad or Mom, too!</u> Blossom Valley Press, PO Box 13378, Tucson, AZ. 85732-3378

36. <u>Divorce Book for Parents, Helping Your Children Cope with Divorce and its Aftermath</u>, V. Lansky

37. <u>For the Sake of the Children: How to Share Your Children with your Ex-Spouse in Spite of your Anger</u>, K. Kline & S. Pew

38. <u>Kids First: Children coping with Divorce and Family Conflict</u>, C. Muklewicz

39. <u>Healing Hearts: Helping Children and Adults Recover from Divorce</u>, E. Hickey

40. <u>Parents are Forever: A Step-by-Step Guide to Becoming Successful Co-Parents after Divorce</u>, S. Thomas

41. <u>What about the Kids?:</u> Judith Wallerstein and Sandra Blakeslee

42. <u>The Truth About Children and Divorce:</u> Robert E. Emery

43. <u>Good Parenting Through Your Divorce</u>: Mary Ellen Hannibal

44. <u>Helping Your Kids Cope with Divorce the Sandcastles Way</u>: M. Gary Neuman and Patricia Romanowski

45. Family Communication, Inc. Books:

    a) <u>Helping Children with Divorce Let's Talk About It</u>: <u>Divorce</u>, Fred Rogers

    b) <u>Let's Talk About It: Step families</u>, Fred Rogers

    c) <u>Mister Rogers Talks with Parents</u>, Fred Rogers and Barry Head

    d) <u>Mister Rogers Talks with Families About Divorce</u>, Fred Rogers and Clare O'Brien

Books for 3 to 5 Year Olds

46. <u>Mommy and Daddy are Divorced</u>, Patricia Perry & Marietta Lynch

47. <u>Sometimes a Family has to Split Up</u>, Jane Werner Watson, Robert E. Switzer and J. Cotter Hirschberg

Books for 6 to 9 Year Olds

48. <u>Dinosaur's Divorce</u>, Laurene Kransy Brown & Marc Brown

49. <u>Families</u>, Meredith Tax

50. <u>Changing Families: A Guide for Kids and Grown-ups,</u> David Passler, Michele Lash, and Sally Blakeslee Ives

51. <u>My Mother's House, My Father's House</u>, C.B. Christiansen

Books for 10 to 12 Year Olds

52. <u>Always, Always</u>, Crescent Dragonwood

53. <u>Why are We Getting a Divorce</u>, Peter Mayle

54. <u>Don't Make Me Smile</u>, Barbara Park

55. <u>It's Not the End of the World</u>, Judy Blume

56. <u>How Does it Feel When Your Parents Get Divorced</u>, Terry Berger

Books for 13 to 17 Year Olds

57. <u>Ask Anybody</u>, Constance Green

58. <u>When Mom and Dad Divorce</u>, Steven L. Nickman

59. <u>The Boys and Girls Book about Divorce</u>, Richard A. Gardner

60. <u>What's Going to Happen to Me?</u>, Eda Lashan

Web Sites

61. <u>www.spig.clara.net</u> Shared Parenting Information Group, promoting responsible shared parenting after separation and divorce.

62. <u>www.divorce.net/coparent.html</u> Decrease the stress of your divorce. (Sample of a co-parenting agreement)

63. <u>www.divorcesource.com</u> Comprehensive divorce information and advice relating to custody, visitation, child support and other issues related to children and divorce.

64. <u>www.ncoff.gse.upenn.edu</u> The Co-Parenting Library.

65. <u>www.betterdivorce.com</u> Parenting and other information on divorce.

66. <u>www.kidsinthemiddle.com</u> Information on the effects of divorce on children.

67. <u>www.flying-solo.com</u> Divorce information for individuals and parents.

68. www.divorcecentral.com Offers resources, state-by-state laws, divorce bookstore.

69. www.DivorceAsFriends.com Tips on avoiding conflict, resolving issues, and keeping divorce attorneys at bay. Suggests ground rules for peaceful divorce.

70. www.DivorceDirectory.com Links to 127 Web sites on divorce.

71. www.DivorceWithoutWar.com Information on mediation services.

72. www.extension.umn.edu/parentsforever Co-Parenting plans

73. www.nolo.com Parenting Agreement

74. http://alaska.net/~akctlib/forms.htm Co-Parent Agreement

75. ShareKids.com and Yahoo.com On-Line Calendars

76. http://www.OurFamilyWizard.com Web site calendar

77. http://www.divorce-education.com Children in the Middle Online Interactive Divorce Programs for Parents.

78. American Bar Association Family Law Section, http://www.abanet.org/family/

79. Centers for Youth and Families: www.youthandfamilies.org

80. The Parent Center: www.parentcenter.com

Audio Programs

81. Building Self-Esteem in Your Child, How to Give Your Child a Healthy Foundation for Life, Career Track,

www.careertrack.com.

RESOURCES

A. Chapter I

Academy of Family Mediators, 1993; The California Dispute Resolution Council; David Grappo, Attorney, Oakland, Ca.; <u>Black's Law Dictionary, Second Pocket Edition</u>, Bryan A. Garner, Editor, West Group; <u>California Rules of Court,</u> Rule 1580 (c); <u>Divorce Mediation: Readings</u>, American Bar Association, Leonard L. Riskin, Editor; <u>The Mediation Process</u>, Christopher W. Moore, Jossey-Bass Publishers, San Francisco; Brian James, "<u>What is Divorce Mediation,</u>" © Resourceful Internet Solutions, Inc.; and, Handbook on Mediation, American Arbitration Association (2006), Thomas E. Carbonneau.

B. Chapter 2

California Practice Guide: Family Law, 2009, Chapter 1:389; The Coalition for Cooperative Divorce (CCD) Workshop, June 2000

C. Chapter 3

<u>A Judge's Guide to Divorce: Uncommon Advice from the Bench</u>, Roderic Duncan; Lynn Brenner, "A Saner Smarter Way to Say Goodbye"; Wendy Landes, "Through the Eyes of Children," Family Law News, Issue 2, Vol. 30, No. 2; ADR Standing Committee Presents a Panel of "Adult Children of Divorce," <u>Family Law News</u>, Issue 2, 2008, Vol. 30, No. 2

D. Chapter 4

Kendall C. Reed, "The Art of Mediation: Ten Rules for Effective Participation; Sharon Ellison, M.S., "Powerful Non-Defensive Communication"; Susan Allison, <u>Conscious Divorce</u> (2001); and, Diane C. Shearer, M.A., CFLE, "Five Critical Questions Divorce Mediators Should Ask" (Family Mediation News).

E. Chapter 5

"In What kind of Case will Mediation Fail?" Art Lieberman, Ph.D.

Colorado Ombuds Office, http://www.colorado.edu/ombuds/graphics/mediation.html

F. Chapter 6

David Grappo, "Active Process," San Francisco Daily Journal, January 24, 2001 Alaska Judicial Council Publication: "A Consumer Guide to Selecting a Mediator," State Justice Institute

G. Chapter 7

<u>Furia v. Helm</u> (2003) 111 CA4th 955, 4 CR3rd 365; <u>California Practice Guide</u> (2009) 1:92; <u>The California Rules of Court</u> 1620-1622; <u>California Evidence Code</u> 703.5 and 1152.

"Mediator Neutrality," Rachel Fishman Green, Esq.

H. Chapter 8

California Practice Guide (2009), The Rutter Group, 8:111-112; Rutter Group, California Family Law Report, "Date of Separation and its Effects"

I. Chapter 9

California Practice Guide: Family Law (2009), The Rutter Group, 8:5, 8:16, 8:20-24, 8:30, 8:71, 8-125-354, 8:535

J. Chapter 10

Stanley L. Bartelmie, "Deferring the Sale of the Family Residence, A.C.F.L.S. Newsletter, Fall 2009, No. 3;

K. Chapter 11

In re Marriage of Hug (1984) 154 Cal.App. 3d 780, 201 CR 676; In re Marriage of Harrison (1986) 179 Cal.App. 3d 1216; 225 CR 234; In re Marriage of Judd (1977) 68 Cal.App.3d 515, 131 CR 246; California Practice Guide: Family Law (2009) The Rutter Group, 8:1245-1257;

L. Chapter 12

Your Divorce Advisor, Diana Mercer; "10 Tips on Personal Property," Marsha Kline Pruett; In re Marriage of Cream (1993), 13 CA4th 81, 16 CR2d 575:

"The Down and Dirty of the Settlement Officer Conference: Common Situations in Settlement Officer Conferences and Alternative Methods of Property Division," James Frederic Cox, Edward F. Mills, Santa Clara County Superior Court.

M. Chapter 13

California Practice Guide: Family Law (2009) The Rutter Group, 6:293-294, 7:173, 7:310-311, 7:340, &:357-360, 7:370-407.

www.extension.umn.edu/parentsforever;

http://www.alaska.net/~akctlib/forms.htm; www.nolo.com (parenting agreement); ShareKids.com; http://www.divorce-education.com; Donald T. Saponsnek, "What Should We Tell the Children? Developing a Mutual Story of the Divorce" (Mediate.com, articles) www.mediate.com/dsaponsnek; Florence Bienenfeld, PhD, "Helping Your Child Succeed After the Divorce"

Melinda Sacks, San Jose Mercury News, Staff Writer, "Mediation Becomes a Key Way to Heal Children of Divorce,"

Donna Leigh Yanish, "Raising Kids Together When Parents are Apart"

Michelle Quinn, "Parents can help ease their children through divorce," San Jose Mercury News, November 10, 2004.

"From Parent Wars to Co-Parenting," Michelle H. Cauly, JaNan Davis, and Marcia Barnes.

N. Chapter 14

California Family Code Sections 4050-4065; California Family Code Sections 4320-4326; Lester, 61-1, USTC 9463, 366US299, 81 SCT 1343; F.T.B. Publication 737: "Tax Information for Registered Domestic Partners"; F.T.B. Publication Q & A: "What if I'm a Domestic Partner"; F.T.B. Publication 2429: "Alimony Frequently Asked Questions"

O. Chapter 15

"How Does Mediation Work?" Jessica A. Stepp (Mediate.com, articles)

"What is Divorce Mediation?" Brian James, July 2007 (Mediate.com, articles)